Four Centuries of Devon Dialect

as recorded in print

by

Lois Lamplugh

ISBN 0 9535321 1 9

A CIP catalogue record for this book is obtainable from the British Library.

Printed by West Somerset Free Press
5 Long Street, Williton, Taunton,
Somerset TA4 4QN

Text prepared by Dennis Hain, 101 Newport Road, Barnstaple.

Published by R M Young (Bookseller)
17 Broad Street, South Molton
N Devon EX36 3AQ

About the Author

Lois Lamplugh grew up in the village of Georgeham. During the Second World War she served in the ATS and afterwards joined the editorial staff of Jonathan Cape. Following the birth of her second child she and her husband, Lawrence Carlile Davis - who is also a Devonian - moved back to the West Country. During the 1970's Lois obtained an honours degree from the Open University, and also taught for some years at a school for maladjusted boys.

She has written more than a dozen books for children, mostly for the older age group and with North Devon settings, and several works of local history. Her biography of Henry Williamson, A Shadowed Man, was published in 1990.

Author's Acknowledgements

I would like to express my thanks to The Devonshire Association for their encouragement and for making a grant towards research expenses. I've also been grateful for the helpfulness of staff at the West Country Studies Library, Exeter, the North Devon Athenaeum and North Devon Record Office, and the Local Studies Centre, Barnstaple.

Books by Lois Lamplugh:

The Stream Way
(impressions of the village of Georgeham in the Thirties)

For older children

The Rifle House Friends
Sean's Leap
The Winter Donkey
Falcon's Tor

For younger children

The Fur Princess and the Fir Prince
Sandrabbit

Local history

Barnstaple: Town on the Taw
A History of Ilfracombe
Minehead and Dunster
Take off from Chivenor
Lundy: Island without equal
A Book of Georgeham and the North West Corner of Devon
Two Rivers Meeting

Biography

A Shadowed Man: Henry Williamson 1895-1977

Numerous smaller works have been written, including a short biography of Parson Jack Russell of Swimbridge, available from R M Young (Bookseller)

Four Centuries of Devon Dialect
as recorded in print

Contents

Chapter One

Early 17th Century: a Devonshire character on the London Stage

In earlier centuries, before anything that could be called Standard English had developed, people in all classes of society would have spoken with some degree of regional accent. Even if it was less pronounced in the speech of the educated — and ladies of the gentry and aristocracy perhaps affected pronunciation and vocabulary far removed from those of their servants and estate workers — men in general seem to have been content to let the way they spoke reveal their county of origin.

The Devon voices of great Tudor seaman-adventurers were heard at court. William Hawkins of Plymouth, the father of the better-known Sir John and grandfather of Sir Richard Hawkins, made three voyages to the coasts of Brazil, 'a thing in those dayes very rare, especially to our Nation', said Hakluyt. On the second voyage, one of the kings of the country asked to be taken to England. Hawkins agreed, and in due course the king arrived in London and was presented to Henry VIII. Everyone at court was amazed to see that the Brazilian's cheeks had holes in which bones had been inserted; moreover a hole in his lower lip had a precious stone in it. After a year, Hawkins set sail for Brazil again, taking the king with him, but unfortunately the latter died on the voyage.

It may be assumed that neither Hawkins nor, later, Drake and Raleigh at the court of Elizabeth I, spoke with anything but the accents of their native county. Other Devonians who must at some time have been called to appear before the queen were the brothers from Northam, Stephen and William Borough. After hazardous voyages in the service of the Muscovy Company, they both held important naval posts: Stephen as Chief Pilot of England and one of the four Masters of Ordnance of the navy, and William as Treasurer of the navy. Their speech too probably retained a strong west country flavour throughout their lives. Not only the maritime but also the mercantile world of London would quite often have heard Devon voices, especially those of merchants in the wool trade. One of the most successful of these was Peter Blundell of Tiverton (1520-1601). He amassed a huge fortune, and left large benefactions to London hospitals and city companies, as well as to various institutions in Tiverton and Exeter. Blundell's School, founded in Tiverton in 1604, remains as his notable memorial,

In spite of all this, it comes as somewhat of a surprise when, in scene six of the fourth act of 'King Lear', Edgar, the son of the Earl of Gloucester, disguised as a peasant, suddenly begins to speak in what is apparently intended as a Devonshire accent. Oswald, Goneril's steward, is about to kill Gloucester. Edgar interposes. Oswald, addressing him as 'bold peasant', orders him to let go of Gloucester's arm. A short exchange follows:

Edgar: Chill not let go, zir, without vurther 'casion.

Oswald: Let go, slave, or thou diest!

Edgar: Good gentleman, go your gait, and let poor volk pass. And chud ha' been zwaggered out of my life, 'twould not ha' been zo long as tis by a vortnight. Nay, come not near the old man; keep out, che vor ye, or ise try whether your costard or my ballow be the harder: chill be plain with you.

Oswald: Out, dunghill!

Edgar: Chill pick your teeth, zir: come; no matter vor your foins.

They fight. Having fatally wounded Oswald, Edgar reverts to his normal way of speaking. (A costard was a kind of apple, sometimes used to mean head; a ballow, in some editions bat, was a cudgel, and foins were thrusts.)

The 'ch' sound at the beginning of words such as 'chill' and 'chud', harking back to the Teutonic 'ich', lingered in the counties that had made up the Saxon Wessex for a surprisingly long time; it may still be found in printed works as late as the 19th century.

When Shakespeare wrote 'King Lear' he was forty-one years old, at the height of his powers. His acting career, which had continued in tandem with his dramatic work, was apparently at an end. The company of actors to which he belonged had had a succession of aristocratic patrons, but in 1603, after the accession of James I, who loved the theatre, it was honoured with the title 'The King's Men', and often performed at court. The company presented 'King Lear' before the king at Whitehall on the night of December 6th, 1606. (It was entered on the Stationers' Register in November, 1607)

It seems possible that royal patronage stimulated Shakespeare's creative energies; between 1603 and 1607 he completed 'All's Well that Ends Well', 'Measure for Measure', 'Othello' and 'Macbeth', as well as 'King Lear'. However, a far less noteworthy play, 'The London Prodigal', appeared with his name on the title page in 1605. It continued to be attributed to him from the time of the Third Folio of 1684 — which included seven other spurious plays — until the 18th century. It was even included in Alexander Pope's edition of 1725. From then on, scholars began to realise its apocryphal nature. It reads like a feeble parody of Shakespeare in his weakest comic vein. Yet it has an interest for Devonians because one of its characters is Oliver, a Devonshire clothier, who has a fairly large part in the semi-farcical twists and turns of the plot.

The London prodigal is Matthew Flowerdale, a spendthrift, gambler and brawler, who repeatedly offers worthless assurances that he will repay the money he borrows from anyone unwary enough to lend it to him. When his father, a merchant, who has been abroad (to Venice, as it happens) returns and receives from his brother a report of Matthew's dissolute behaviour, he disguises himself as a serving man and is taken on by Matthew — who in the tradition of farce fails to recognise his own father. The main action of the play concerns the attempt of Sir Lancelot Spurcock to marry off his three daughters, Frances, Luce and Delia. Frances, who is vain and empty-headed, attracts a husband without difficulty; Delia has refused seven apparently worthy suitors, and Sir Lancelot is resigned to her remaining single. However, Luce has three suitors: Sir Arthur Greenfield, an army commander, Matthew Flowerdale and Oliver. Sir Lancelot favours the latter, describing him as

'The De'enshire lad

A wary fellow, marry full of wit,

And rich by the rood.'

Clearly it is his wealth that is especially in his favour. Recommending him to Luce, her father urges her to

'. . . look on this De'enshire lad;

Fair, fat and lovely, both in purse and person.'

To this Oliver responds, 'Well, Zir, cham as the lord made me. You know me well ivin; cha have threescore pack of kersey at Blackenhall, and chief credit bezides; and my fortune may be zo good as another's zo it may.'

With Matthew, who has mocked his accent and his occupation, he has already had a disagreement, and threatened to fight him (' . . . che would 'a given thee zutch a whisterpoop under the ear, che would made thee vanged another (sic) at my veet.') This seems to give Flowerdale senior the ludicrous idea that Matthew may be brought to his senses by a spell in prison if he is arrested for duelling with Oliver; still posing as Matthew's servant, he delivers a challenge to Oliver, who accepts willingly ('Zirrah, zirrah, an 'twere not an old fellow, and sent after an errant (errand), child give thee something, but chud be no money: but hold thee, for I zee thou art somewhat testern (i.e. in need of money): hold thee, there's vorty shillings: bring thy master a-veeld, chil give thee vorty more. Look, thou bring him, tell him; chil mar his dancing tressels; chil use him, he was ne'er zo used since his dame bound his head; chil mar him for capering any more, che vore thee.' When Sir Lancelot tries to dissuade him, he says 'What do you think, chil be abaffled up and down the town for a messel and a scoundrel? No che vore you. Zirrah, chil come; zay no more; chil come, tell him.' Waiting alone at the appointed place, he tells himself, 'If 'a come, zo; if 'a come not, zo. And che were avise he would make a coystrel (a coystrel was a low, mean man) ched veeze him, ched vang him in hand; che would hoyst him, and give it to him to and again, zo chid.'

Meanwhile Sir Lancelot has been deceived into thinking that Matthew is heir to a fortune and forced the unfortunate Luce — who favours the soldierly Sir Arthur — to marry him. Immediately after the ceremony Sir Lancelot learns that he has been conned, and tries to get Matthew arrested, whereupon Luce, while admitting that she was compelled to marry against her will, defies her father: 'I must not leave my husband in distress. Now I must comfort him, not go with you.'

He tells her that if she goes so she must

'Never come near my sight, nor look to me;

Call me not father, look not for a groat.'

Old Flowerdale's brother now has Matthew arrested for debt, but Luce successfully pleads for his release, promising to raise the money somehow. Her reward is to be told by Matthew

'. . . get you gone to the greasy chuff, your father, bring me your dowry, or never look on me.' When she exclaims, 'Alas, what shall I do?' he suggests

'Why, turn whore; that's a good trade

And so perhaps I'll see thee now and then,'

Old Flowerdale takes care of her (as well he might, given that it is his absurd plot that has brought about her marriage to his scapegrace son).

She next appears dressed as a Dutchwoman and acting as serving maid to her sister Frances (who of course does not recognise her). Matthew arrives at the house of Frances and her husband. He has been begging in the street, having gambled away the money given him; he has even tried to rob Delia, being prevented by the sturdy Oliver. He hopes to cajole the 'Dutch frow' into stealing silver and jewels from the house. Sir Lancelot arrives and accuses Matthew of murdering Luce; at this she throws off her disguise and, taking saintly forbearance to the verge of idiocy, says she will yield to her husband 'My love, my duty and my humbleness'. With startling suddenness this causes him to become a reformed character. Calling her 'wonder among wives', he claims that

'Thy chastity has infused

Another soul in me.'

Everyone takes him at his word, except Sir Lancelot, and even he is eventually persuaded. Finally Oliver asks if he may marry Delia, having lost Luce, but she says, 'Husbands, however good, I will have none. He answers

'Why, then, che will live a bachelor too. Che zet not a vig by a wife, if a wife zet not a vig by me.'

The play ends with the whole company cheerfully going off to dinner.

This knockabout piece gives the impression of having been cobbled together in a hurry to meet the deadline of some special performance; (it is incidentally by no means the only play attributed to Shakespeare during his lifetime and for some considerable period afterwards; others include 'Locrine', 'The Puritan', 'Fair Em' and 'Mucidorous') The identity of the author of 'The London Prodigal' will probably never be discovered, though quite a few people at the time must have known it, especially members of the King's Men who, as the title page shows, performed it. Certainly Shakespeare would have known the writer, who may well have asked for help in shaping or editing it. One or two of the speeches, particularly those of the unfortunate Luce — doubly betrayed by the avarice of her father and of the man he forces her to marry — have a faint echo of Shakespeare's voice. And he can hardly have resented the action of Nicholas Butter in publishing the play as by William Shakespeare, as it was Butter who brought out 'King Lear' just two years later.

It is worth noting that at one point there is a suggestion that the unknown author was working, without enthusiasm, on a plot foisted upon him by someone else; he gives Matthew the line ' . . . I'd gladly know if a man might not have a foolish plot out of Master Oliver to work upon'. This sounds like an in joke: was there a man called Oliver known to the actors and perhaps to the audience?

The actor playing Oliver was probably able to get quite a few laughs out of the part. His Devonshire accent may have been regarded as funny in itself, though he may only have been capable of using some sort of stage Mummerset. How close to the true Devon dialect of the time Oliver's speeches come it is of course impossible to tell. The writer provided some help in pronunciation, such as the traditional 'v' for initial 'f' and 'z' for initial 's'. On hearing that Sir Lancelot has forced Luce to marry Matthew, Oliver says, 'Ay, ha' the old vellow zarved me thick a trick? why, man, he was a promise, chil chud 'a had her: is 'a zutch a vox: chil look to his water, che vore him.' ('Che vore him' evidently means 'I warn him', as Edgar's 'che vore ye' in 'King Lear' means 'I warn you.') Later Oliver uses 'ich' on its own: 'Well, cha 'a bin zarved many a sluttish trick, but zutch a lerripoop as thick ich was never zarved.' When he first falls out with Matthew he says, 'Well. zir, though you vlouten cloth and kersey, chet 'a seen zutch a kersey coat wear out the town sick a silkin jacket as thick a one you wear.' whereupon Matthew makes fun of him with 'Well said, vlitten vlatten.'

Oliver's dialect is largely a matter of pronunciation. To have introduced many dialect words unfamiliar to a London audience would have been counter-productive. However there are a few that evidently belonged principally to Devon. 'Vang', for instance, used here in the sense of both to strike and to take, appears in 19th century glossaries as to take (though one writer has 'to stick close to'). 'Whisterpoop', too, had a long life, as did 'vease' for squeeze. Once or twice Oliver uses 'messel', which appears in Chaucer to mean leper, in the sense of scoundrel, and a character in the 18th century 'Exmoor Courtship' uses 'meazle' apparently in the same sense, but the word is not included in 19th century dialect works.

As has been said, the King's Men had a number of aristocratic patrons during the reign of Elizabeth, and the queen herself often watched them act. During the 1590s they sometimes left London to go on tour, visiting Faversham, Dover, Rye, Bristol and Bath. With the accession of James I in 1603 they often performed at court by command of the king, who loved theatrical entertainments of all kinds, and gave the company a new patent, which licensed them to play in any town or university. Their leaders, who would have included Shakespeare, became Grooms of the Bedchamber, and thus sworn members of the royal household. Again they went on tour, visiting Oxford several times, as well as Shrewsbury and Coventry. Between 1605 and the Christmas of 1607 they acted at Maidstone and Dunwich.[2] And in that year of 1607 an entry in the borough accounts of Barnstaple recorded 'Given to ye Kynge's players beynge in town this year Xs.' On this slender evidence it has been suggested that the people of early 17th century Barnstaple saw Shakespeare act.

Unfortunately this is doubtful. Although the *Dictionary of National Biography* says that Shakespeare's career as an actor was probably coming to an end in 1610, his name does not appear on cast lists of productions by the Kings Men after 1603. He was by that time a man of means. He had become the owner of a large house in Stratford-upon-Avon in 1597, and in 1605 he bought half the tithes of that town — a profitable investment. He usually spent some time in Stratford every year (it was after all where his wife and children lived) and it is possible that by 1607 he was unwilling to make the long, tedious journey to north Devon, preferring to concentrate on writing.

Yet when members of the King's Men visited Barnstaple, they would have heard genuine Devon dialect, and possibly met genuine Devon clothiers. They may even have played 'The London Prodigal' to their Devon audience.

The play has little interest except as an example of the sort of not-very-good comedy that the King's Men were sometimes content to perform. Yet the questions it raises remain: not only who wrote it and what were his relations with the company, and indeed with Shakespeare, but whether he had some Devon connections and through his knowledge of the dialect, had been able to influence the inclusion of Edgar's brief 'Devon' speech in 'King Lear'.

Twenty years after 'The London Prodigal' was staged, a Devon-born cleric who had some reputation as a playwright and poet wrote a poem of six eight-line stanzas in dialect. Including it in 'The West Country Garland', an anthology published in 1875, the editor, R.N. Worth, referred to it as 'the earliest example of Devonshire dialect on record', but as has been seen, this was not entirely accurate. However, it does appear to be the first known example of a Devonian of some education deciding to try his hand at versifying in dialect. He was William Strode (1598-1644), a member of the family who lived at Newnham, near Plympton in south Devon. He was related to the Richard Strode who was one of the five members of parliament whom Charles I attempted to arrest in 1641.

In 1625 the king, having declared war on Spain, ordered an army of ten thousand to assemble at Plymouth ready to sail. All kinds of trouble followed — plague, food shortages, and an attempt by desperate men to mutiny. Charles paid the city a visit — presumably before the situation became serious — and stayed there for ten days. (During that time he knighted a man called Bagge who had apparently pocketed most of the money entrusted to him to feed the troops. In parliament, an M.P. referred to him as 'bottomless Bagge'.)

It was Charles' visit which prompted Strode, who, like others of his family, was no royalist, to write his verses, in the form of a letter by a countryman from Dartmoor making his first acquaintance with town life.

'Thou n'ere woot riddle, neighbour John,
Where ich of late have bin-a;
Why ich have bin to Plymouth, man,
The like was yet n'ere zeen-a:
Zich streets, zich men, zich hugeous seas,
Zich things and guns there rumbling;
Thyself, like me, would'st blesse to see
Zich bombination grumbling.

The streets be pight of shingle-stone,
Doe glissen like the sky-a,
The zshops ston ope and all yeere long
I'se think a faire there bee-a,
And many a gallant here goeth
I' goold, that saw the King-a;
The King zome sweare himself was there,
A man or some zich thing-a.'

This last line is perhaps intended to indicate that Strode has no use for the belief in the divine right of kings; Charles is a man like any other.

In the third and fourth stanzas the sea seems to stand as a symbol for the monarchy: it lies lower than the land

'yet all consent
'Twas higher than the Moor
'Tis strange how looking down a cliffe
Men do looke upwards rather.'

He goes on to describe the scene offshore:

'Amidst the water wooden birds,
And flying houses zwim-a;
All full of things as ich ha' heard,
And goods up to ye brim-a;
They goe unto another world,
Desiring to conquiera-a (sic)

Vor wch these guns, voile develish ones
Do dunder and spett vire-a.'

In the final stanza he says he'll no longer 'moape . . . to watch a zheepe or zheene-a' but make for somewhere better (presumably the other world for which the ships are bound):

'Ch'll thither hye, for this place I
Do take in great induggin'.

As can be seen, Strode's use of the first person singular is variable, changing from 'ich' to 'I'se' and finally to I. He has not attempted to introduce specifically dialect words, unless one may count 'bombination' and 'induggin'. His verses are therefore more interesting as an indication of the sort of anti-royalist feeling that Plymouth, and much of the rest of Devon, would show during the Civil War, than as an example of contemporary dialect.

Remarkably — and regrettably — it does not seem that any further writings of this kind, in print or in manuscript, are known to have been produced until the early 18th century, and then the writer was again a Devon-born cleric, though this time from the north of the county.

THE LONDON Prodigall.

As it was plaide by the Kings Maie-
ſties ſeruants.

By *VVilliam Shakeſpeare*,

LONDON.

Printed by T. C. for *Nathaniel Butter*, and
are to be ſold neere *S Auſtins* gate,
at the ſigne of the pyde Bull.
1605.

*Reproduced in The Shakespeare Apocrypha, edited by
C.F. Tucker Brooke (Oxford University Press, 1918)*

Chapter Two

18th Century: Devonshire dialogues from Exmoor and Torrington

The use of the Anglo-Saxon 'ich' in the first half of the 17th century, and its lingering existence in such words as 'chill', 'chud' and so on was not, of course, confined to Devon; it was to be found in neighbouring counties. In the early 1720s Daniel Defoe, travelling westwards on one of the journeys he was to describe in his *Tour of Great Britain*, which came out in three volumes in 1724-26, reached Somerset and complained that the local people's way of expressing themselves was not elsewhere 'in so gross a degree as in this part . . . tho the tongue be all meer natural English, yet those that are but a little acquainted with them, cannot understand one half of what they say.' He was related to a schoolmaster in Martock, who took him into a classroom where a boy was reading aloud. To Defoe's surprise he was saying, 'Chav a doffed my cooat, how shall I don't? Chav a wash'd my veet, how shall I moil 'em?' He was using a Bible of normal text, and the words before him were from the Song of Solomon, v, 3: 'I have put off my coat, how shall I put it on, I have washed my feet, how shall I defile them?

The dextrous dunce, as Defoe put it, was transforming the printed words into his 'country jargon . . . the boorish local speech, called jouring'. (In 19th century glossaries 'jouring ' (spelled 'geowering') is defined as swearing, quarrelling or scolding.)

Not long after Defoe's visit to Martock, an Exeter printer, Andrew Brice, published part one of a dialogue in the Devon dialect entitled, 'An Exmoor Scolding in the Propriety and Decency of Exmoor language, between two sisters.' This appeared anonymously in his 'Weekly Journal' in June, 1727. He brought out part two, or 'Bout the Second', two months later. In June, 1746. a somewhat longer dialogue, 'The Exmoor Courtship, or, a Suitoring Discourse in the Devonshire Dialect and Mode, near the forest of Exmoor' became known to a considerably wider readership when it was included in the influential London-based 'Gentleman's Magazine'. It was sent in by a correspondent who signed himself 'H. Oxon.(it has been suggested that this should be H. Exon.) He said it was written 'by a clergyman of Devonshire, near the forest of Exmoor, but, I believe, has received some additions.' He marked a number of words with an asterisk, asking readers to send in their meaning, 'for I cannot so much as guess at it.' In August, 1746, the magazine also published the 'Exmoor Scolding', and a reader who signed himself 'Devoniensis' responded to the request for definitions, saying that he had lived for a good while within a few miles of the forest of Exmoor, and that the dialect was not that of the whole county; rather improbably, he claimed that it would be 'almost as unintelligible to the southern parts of it, as to a citizen of London.' He pointed out that the 'cham', 'chad' and so on used in the dialogue 'was once the general mode of proper speaking throughout the kingdom, and may be found in many ancient English authors.' The vocabulary he submitted ran to some 170 words.

The apparent appeal of the dialogues was remarkable. There were seven Exeter editions between 1746 and 1771 (Andrew Brice died in 1773) and three more appeared by 1788. The 1771 edition had an anonymous preface and a glossary; this too claimed that 'many words and phrases would not be well understood by people in the south Hams' and that 'none but the lowest class of People generally speak the language here exemplified.' The writer suggested that his explanatory notes and glossary 'may be of some Use, to such lawyers as go the Western Circuit, by whom the evidence of a Country-man is sometimes mistaken for want of a proper Interpretation of his Language'. Referring to the 'objurgatory wenches' of the 'Scolding', he remarked that there were those who would confirm that 'noted Scolds . . . when well match'd with foul-mouthed and nimble-tongued Antagonists' were apt to 'string together a Variety of abusive Words.'

The fame of the 'Courtship' was spread by 'Blackwood's Magazine', which published a portion of it in 1819, while yet another reprint of the 1771 edition was produced in Exeter in 1827.

Various names have been suggested for the author, or authors, of the two dialogues. In an address to the Devonshire Association in 1861 its first president, Sir John Bowring, claimed that his paternal grandfather, Benjamin Bowring, had written them with Andrew Brice. A later suggestion was that Archdeacon Hole of Barnstaple had been the author, but this has been discounted as the future Archdeacon would have been only seventeen in 1727. However his father, the Revd. Joshua Hole of South Molton (1664-1746) was put forward as a more likely candidate. There seems general agreement that the raw material for both the 'Courtship' and the 'Scolding' was supplied by Peter Lock (1688-1728), a blind itinerant fiddler from North Molton. According to the writer of the 1771 preface, Lock's skill as a musician 'recommended him to the Notice of the Great', but he liked to talk to ordinary people, storing up in his memory their phrases and diction, and it was because the 'neighbouring clergyman' put them down on paper and circulated them in manuscript that the dialogues were attributed to him. Yet it is interesting that one of the sons of the Revd Joshua Hole was the Revd John Hole, who from 1724 to 1733 was Latin master at the school in South Molton established by a local benefactor, Hugh Squeir.[1] Could it have been the Revd John Hole, who would have been of much the same age as Peter Lock, who found it amusing to listen to the fiddler's accounts of local dialect usage, and concocted the two dialogues from them? Andrew Brice, of whom it was said that 'his disposition was mirthful', may well have made alterations and additions when the copies came into his possession.

Even without the reference to the Devonshire dialect in the subtitle of the 'Courtship', it would be clear from the mention of Parracombe, Challacombe, 'Moulton' (which may mean North or South Molton, but is almost certainly the latter) and Shirwell Hundred that the setting is the north-east corner of Devon, despite the fact that the greater part of Exmoor is in Somerset. It is in effect a playlet in six short scenes (it would be interesting to know if it was ever staged in, say, South Molton). It has four characters, Andrew Moorman, a young farmer, Margery (always addressed as Magery in the dialogue) Vagwell, his sweetheart, her sister Tamsin and their grandmother, Old Gammer Nell. Andrew is a boisterous suitor and Margery a lively and coquettish girl of eighteen. (Andrew and Margery address one another as 'Cozen Andra' and 'Cozen Magery'. This might be an example of the old use of the word to mean some distant degree of relationship other than the modern one of the sons and daughters of anyone's uncles and aunts. Yet it seems they are literally cousins, as Andrew addresses Margery's grandmother as 'Ount Nell' and Margery refers to his mother as 'Ount Moorman'.)

When Andrew arrives Margery refuses to kiss him, saying that she would 'as leefe kiss the back o' ma hond, as e'er a man in Challacombe, or eet (yet) in Parracombe'. Andrew says he doesn't believe her. A stage direction reads, 'Zwop! he kisses and smuggles her'. He says he has fought a man who said 'an eel word' about Margery, and 'roil'd (railed) zo, that es couldn't bear it.' So, unable to 'zit mumchance' he had 'toz'd en, es lamb'd en, es lac'd en, es thong'd en, es drash'd en, es drumm'd en, es tann'd en.' His opponent had begun by giving him 'a whisterpoop under tha year' (ear) and a 'vulch in tha leer' but Andrew overcame him. Margery thanks him, but hopes his opponent won't 'go vor a warrant vor ye, and take ye bevor the cunsabel' (constable). Andrew is unconcerned. He has a witness who would take his 'corneral oath' that the other man began the fight. 'An zo let un go, and wipe what ha zits upon a Zindeys wi' his warrant.'

There follows another stage direction: 'He takes hold of her, and paddles in her neck and bosom'. She pushes him away and tells him to 'gi' o'er'. He says, ' How skittish we be now! Yew weren't zo skittish wey Kester Hosegood to Daraty Vuzz's up-setting. No, no, yew weren't zo skittish then, ner zo squeamish neither. He purt mully and soully till he was weary.'

Margery denies this forcefully. Andrew, mollified, kisses her and says he hasn't yet told her his 'arrant' (errand). When she asks what it is, he answers, 'Tes this: volus nolus, wut ha' ma?' (It has been suggested that this is dog Latin for 'nolens volens' — willy nilly — heard in a magistrate's court.) Margery pretends not to understand his meaning. He reminds her, unromantically, that he has land at Challacombe and Parracombe, where he needs someone to milk the cow and look after the pigs and 'tha thengs of tha howze'. She points out that a servant could do all that, and is unmoved to be told that the land at Parracombe is worth 'twenty gold nobles a year, and a purse to put them in'. She insists that she wouldn't marry 'the best man in Challacombe, er eet in Parracombe', and tells him that she is going to speak to her sister Tamsin. Scene two shows her excitedly telling Tamsin 'tha banes (banns) wull g' in next Zindey.' She describes Andrew as 'a spicy vella' of twenty-two', but confides that she has told him she wouldn't marry 'the best man in Sherwill-hundered'. Tamsin calls her a 'wicked countervit' and warns her that Andrew might take her at her word and 'come no more anearst tha'. Margery calls her an 'alkitotle' (fool) and assures her that Andrew is not so silly as to believe her. For all that, with the first hint of feeling she has shown, she adds that if the banns are not read by 'Zendey-zenneart' it will 'borst ma heart'.

She returns to Andrew, who has been reading a 'ballet' (ballad), and accuses him of keeping company with a girl to whom she applies a string of derogatory epithets: 'a gurt banging, thonging, muxy drawbreech' and so on. Andrew claims that it is the girl's brother who has spread this story. According to the stage direction, he 'speaks in a great passion and shows with his hands how he'll beat his adversary', saying he'll 'gi' en a lick'. Having listed more than a dozen ways in which he'll attack him, he ends 'chell gi' en a whappet, and a wherret, and a whisterpoop too.' (It is interesting to find the splendid word whisterpoop, used by Oliver in 'The London Prodigal' more than a hundred years earlier, still current.) Finally he says that if folk are jealous before they are married, they will be afterwards, and bids her goodbye. Margery coaxes him back and offers him bread and cheese and cider. They kiss and make up, and Margery suggests that they go to visit her grandmother, who lives nearby.

On arrival at Old Nell's house Andrew politely asks after her health. This enables the writer to provide a list of Devon dialect names for ailments, including a 'glam or two' (sores of some kind), a crick in the niddick (the nape of the neck), an 'allernbatch (old sore), barngun (ringworm) and 'boneshave' (sciatica). However, she says that old Jilian Vrinkle — presumably the local wise woman — has blessed her, and she is better. She has heard that he and Margery are attracted to one another, and gives her approval, assuring him that Margery is not like some 'giglets', all for 'gamboyling" and 'ragrouting', but is a 'tyrant maid for work, and tha stewardest vittest wanch that comath on the stones o' Moulton.'

In an aside, Margery thanks her and, as when speaking to Tamsin, admits that if she couldn't have Andrew, it would burst her heart. Yet aloud she continues to insist that she won't marry. Old Nell calls her to one side and scolds her for not accepting this 'comely sprey vitty vella'. Andrew overhears this and thanks her, adding 'Bet now chave a zeed ye, 'tes so good as chad eat ye' (But now I've seen you, it's as good as if I'd eaten you). He takes his leave. Margery says she may go to see 'Ont' (aunt) Moorman. A brief scene, set in 'The Open Country' shows her going to 'Challacombe-Moor stile', where she knows she'll encounter Andrew. He overtakes her and evidently hugs her tightly, as she tells him to stop 'creeming (squeezing) a body zo' and complains that his beard 'precketh ill-vavourdly'. He asks her if he shall put in the banns next Sunday, 'nolus volus'. She tells him she'll forbid them if he does, but once more he is not convinced that she means it.

In the final scene, once again in Margery's home, Tamsin asks Margery why she is capering, whistling and singing. Margery tells her that her banns will be read on Sunday. Tamsin remarks that they'll be married near together, as her banns have already been read, though 'my man don't eet tell me tha day.' Margery says that she'll go into Moulton to buy canvas for a new apron. Tamsin responds with the mysterious warning that she 'can't tell what may happen to tha in the middle banes'. Their acrimonious parting ends the playlet on this note of uncertainty.

The 'Exmoor Scolding' again shows two sisters, Wilmot Moreman and Thomasin Moreman, supposedly spinning, but in view of their vicious squabbling and frequent threats of physical violence, they don't seem to do much work. They accuse one another of sexual adventures; at the beginning Wilmot is hinting that Thomasin had some kind of venereal disease since she was seventeen. Thomasin furiously challenges her to be more specific, and counters that 'the crime o' tha country' (local gossip) has it that when Wilmot lived 'up to tha cot, tha wert old Roger Hill's under bed-blonket' ('an' sounds repeatedly appear as 'on' in both the 'Courtship' and the 'Scolding'). In a typical exchange, Thomasin says 'How! ya gurt, chounting, grumbling, glumping, zower-zwaped, yerring trash!' and Wilmot replies, 'Don't tell me o' glumping: oll the neighbourhooden know thee to be a ve-aking, blazing, tiltish hussey.'

Finally Wilmot starts pulling her sister's hair. Thomasin shouts for help, complaining that she is being strangled by her bonnet string ('Her hath a chuck'd ma wi' tha chingstey'). Old Julian Moreman comes in and tells them to be quiet ('Labbe, labbe, soze, labbe', i.e. let be. 'Soze' or more usually 'soce' was a friendly term used both by people of the same sex and of opposite sexes; the equivalent might be 'mate' or 'dear'). He grumbles that from 'candle-douting to candle-teening' they are always quarrelling. The writer manages to cram in no fewer than fifteen pairs of words for their disputes, from 'agging or veaking, gawing or sherking' to 'blogging or glumping, rearing or snapping'.

It is a disagreeable piece, mercifully a good deal shorter than the 'Courtship'. Where there is some movement and variety in the latter, the 'Scolding' is static, and monotonous in the crude vituperation exchanged by the sisters.

The eminent west country dialect scholar and philologist, Frederic Elworthy, (1830-1907), appears to have taken the subtitle of the 'Scolding' literally, whereas it is surely ironic; he considered that to claim the dialogue as 'a fair sample of the propriety or decency of the young women of the district in the last century is simply scandalous'. In 1879 he published a version of the two dialogues, 'The original texts edited, collated and arranged, with a complete transcript in Glossic, the vocabulary enlarged, and the whole illustrated with copious notes'. He seemed to think some apology for doing so was necessary, at least as far as the 'Scolding' was concerned. Attributing the 'utter foulness of much of the dialogue' to its clerical author, he added that 'nothing but the confidence that its form is not such as to attract the ordinary reader, and that students alone will take the trouble to wade through it, would have induced me to touch such pitch.' This is somewhat contradictory; in a paper read to the Devonshire Association in 1880 he said that the dialogues 'may be bought in about the fiftieth edition, at the booksellers, for sixpence' and elsewhere said that they were available at station bookstalls.

A gentler and more loving courtship dialogue was written about the middle of the 18th century by Mary Palmer, an older sister of Sir Joshua Reynolds. According to a biographer of Reynolds, 'The literature and philosophy which they found at home, imparted with a strong Devonshire accent, must have influenced not only Sir Joshua and Fanny's leanings towards the literary and artistic life, but also his sister Mary's aptitude for reducing local manners and customs into the terms of dialect conversations. Joshua himself became an authority on the Devon dialect . . . while Mary's dialogue is acknowledged as a minor classic of its kind.'[2] (Fanny was another of the Reynolds siblings, who remained unmarried; she had a minor talent as a painter.)

Their mother came from Torrington, which may explain how it was that Mary married John Palmer of that town, a lawyer by profession and a wealthy landowner, who was three times mayor. He built himself a fine large house opposite the church in 1752.

Mary Palmer died in 1794, at the age of seventy-eight. In 1837 one of her grandsons, James Palmer, a doctor who emigrated to Australia and was later knighted, published 'A Dialogue in the Devonshire Dialect, in three parts, by a Lady', which he said had been written about the middle of the 18th century. It was an incomplete version of his grandmother's work. It is possible that Mary Palmer had read the 'Exmoor Scolding' and 'Exmoor Courtship' when they appeared in the 'Gentleman's Magazine' in 1746, and decided to produce some dialogues of a rather different kind. It would appear that her daughter, Mrs Gwatkin, took exception to her nephew's decision to bring out his imperfect version of the 'Dialogues'. In 1839 she published 'A Devonshire Dialogue in Four Parts'; her prefatory note explained that this had been handed about in manuscript to interested readers (which recalls the way the Exmoor dialogues had been circulated) and extracts had been 'inserted in various publication', often without acknowledgement. Referring to John Palmer's edition, without naming him, she said she had been 'induced to publish the *whole* from the original manuscript in her possession.'

The list of characters includes John Hogg, a farmer; his wife, always referred to as Dame; Betty, his servant maid; Bat, an apprentice boy, and

Robin, Betty's sweetheart. Although Betty and Robin have the only speaking parts, Hogg, Dame and Bat are the subject of much of their talk. There is also a nature loving parson, who talks to trees, releases birds from snares and pays boys to free butterflies they have caught — and is therefore regarded by Robin and most of his parishioners as mazed. He lends Mrs Hogg books, which Betty, to her delight, is allowed to read.

John Hogg is a domestic tyrant, with a vicious temper; he repeatedly rants at his submissive wife, is often drunk, and is apt to throw out food uneaten because he is dissatisfied with it. Bat is one of the unhappy pauper children who, under the Elizabethan Poor Law, then still in force, were apprenticed to farmers at the age of seven or eight and bound until they were twenty-one. With a master such as John Hogg they were in effect child slaves, ill-treated, overworked and half-starved. Betty, who claims to stand up to Hogg, does her best to comfort the boy; she tries to teach him to read, and hears him say his prayers.

The first dialogue begins with Robin leaping over a stile and greeting Betty with 'Zo, Bet, how is't? How de try?' Similarly in the 'Exmoor Courtship' Margery asks Andrew 'Hoh! cozen Andra, how d'ya try?' and Andrew salutes old Gammer Nell with 'Good den, good den, ount Nell. Well, how d'ye try?' Since there is no reason to suppose that Mary Palmer copied this form of greeting from the 'Courtship', it was probably much used as a form of 'How are you?' in rural Devon at this time. Robin is not at work because it is the day of the village Revel, the annual celebration, usually on Whit Monday, which was a feature of Devon life generally for centuries. He asks Betty why she took no notice of him when they were in the crowd coming out of church the previous day, 'Rail Zinday' (Revel Sunday). She says that her mistress 'can't abide sich may-games and high-de-lows Sabbath days. Gracious! what a hurly-burly 'twas! How the volks veased out o' church — higgledy-piggledy, helter skelter: zich jitting, driving and dringing. I thort no other, but I shou'd be squat to death. I'll never go to church of a Rail Zinday again, I'll be bound vor't . . . Our seat was so full as it cou'd cram, when who shou'd come in but Joice Jollard, and Ruth Rumpsom, so red as two roost cocks, tittering, and vanning wi' their hats, as thof 'twas cruel buldering, quelstering weather...' Robin remarks that that was to show 'their high-peak'd loady heads, wi'a wallage o'hair, plastered with mort and flour, bevore, and a thumping nug behind, bedizze'd with rory tory ribbons, like garters hang'd up in a vair, and thingembob in their ears.' When Betty answers that 'Why, good now, that's the tip of the mode. I'm told that they join vor a red book, that tells 'em the fashion: what dost think o' that?' he says, 'Their bacon faces ban't vit to play tricks way. I heard an old 'oman zay, her long'd to gee 'em a good scat in the chaps . . . If you had but zeed 'em, when they com'd out o' church, colting and giggling like two hobby-horses, with their pie-picked, skittering, flimsy gowns, vagging in the wind or reeping in the mux.'

This passage, with its doubling or trebling of more of less synonymous verbs and adjectives, is somewhat reminiscent of the language of the 'Courtship' and 'Scolding', although less insistent on piling up words of similar meaning. Definitions of dialect words are given as footnotes, and are repeated in a glossary at the end, provided by a vicar at Modbury. Using this, the passage may be rendered in part: 'How the people hurried out of church, higgledy-piggledy, helter skelter: such pushing, driving and squeezing. I thought I'd be crushed to death. I'll never go to church on Revel Sunday again, I'll be bound. Our seat was as full as it could be, when who should come in but Joice Jollard and Ruth Rumpsom, as red as two roosters, tittering and fanning themselves with their hats as though it was hot, sultry weather . . . to show their high-piled heads, with a lump of hair, plastered with lard and flour, at the front, and a great bunch behind, bedizzened with gaudy ribbons, like garters hanging up at a fair, and thingamabobs in their ears . . . If you'd only seen them, when they came out of church, frolicking and giggling like two hobby-horses, with their piebald, skittering flimsy gowns, flapping in the wind, or trailing in the mud.'

The congregation can be seen tramping away across the 'arrish' (stubble) on their way to the Revel, the 'crowder', the local fiddler, with them, and Robin asks Betty to go with him to watch the 'wraxling' (wrestling) and take part in the dancing competition. (The west country form of wrestling, a usual part of village revels, was a very rough sport. In both Devon and Cornwall kicking was allowed: the ugly aspect of this game was this shin-hacking with steel-tipped boots, so that the legs of the struggling men would often stream with blood, and to be laced from knee to ankle with blue scars was the normal mark of a wrestler.)

Betty answers that she has many chores to do, and then will be going to visit her 'old gonmar' at Thatchcott. Robin goes with her in the afternoon. On the way Betty gives him a detailed account of John Hogg's heartless behaviour to his wife and the boy Bat (he even kicks the dog when it goes towards him wagging its tail). When they reach Thatchcott there is no one at home. Robin says that the old folks will have gone to the Revel. (At this point in John Palmer's edition a passage is missing.)

Robin now tries to tell Betty that he loves her, but she is unwilling to listen — not, evidently, from mere coquettishness, like Margery in the 'Courtship', but because she is genuinely uncertain of her feelings. However, he takes her hand and insists that he won't let go until she has heard him out. 'I don't know what I do, or what I zay. Oh! Bet, thee can't think what a way I be in; many, many nearts (nights) I han't teen'd (closed) my eyes vor thinking o' thee. I can't live zo, 'tis ne'er the ne'er (sic — according to Sir John Bowring, this means 'to no purpose') to tell o 'et. I must make an end o' et, zome way or t'other, I'm bent upon't; therefore no shilly-shally — but look there, thee zeest the sin yonder, a'most a heal'd (covered or hidden) by thicka hill; now, if thee doesn't zay thee wot ha' me, bevore 'tis quite clean and sheer a'gone out o' sight, zure, and zure, and double zure, I will ne'er ax thee again, but go a solger (soldier) and ne'er zee thee more.'

At this Betty begins to weep, and tells him she is 'a poor moody-hearted timersome body, and you scare one zo . . . If I say is (yes), I may be sorry, and if I say no, I may be sorry too.' When Robin assures her that he'll work for her, 'vor thee I could spend my heart's blood; every thing shall be as thee wot ha' et,' she says, 'If it's ordain'd I shall ha' thee, I wol try to make thee a good wife.'

They part, agreeing to meet the next morning after milking. John Palmer's edition ends at this unsatisfactory and inconclusive point, making it understandable that Mrs Gwatkin was anxious to present the complete version — almost twice the length of Palmer's — to the public.

In the third dialogue Robin makes a definite proposal: he wants to 'put in the banns next Zinday' but Betty is full of anxiety about 'Dame': 'Zure Rab, I can't think of leaving her it (yet) awhile. Wan, that's always ailing, lacketh some tender-hearted body about her. What will her do when I be ago? Her's is a lonesome life.'

Robin says that he has 'a huge kindness vor Dame, as well as you; but think 'pon poor me too — Zimmeth her breaketh apace?' Betty agrees that she has never been the same since the death of her little boy. 'Her life was bound up in en . . . How it cut me to the heart to zee her when a' died.'

Hearing that Betty might leave her, Mrs Hogg has wished her well but warned her that 'married life is a life of trial', and her husband, with characteristic rancour, has accused Betty of only wanting to marry Robin because he expects to inherit money his father has worked hard to save up. Robin angrily refutes this, and wonders that she can put up with the man's bullying. She says, 'Vormerly when a' used to snap and swear at me, I used to cry like any thing; but now I told en, flat and plain, that I didn't meend his flouts and his jeers . . . as a' was my Measter, I'd try to weather it out. 'Tis but a little while, and when I'm ago, I shall ne'er hanker to zit my voot over the drekstool (threshold) o' his door again, I'll be warnes (I'll warrant); if et wasn't vor Dame, I never wid, but vor her I could lie down my life.'

Robin has the solution; he knows of a house to let 'wher the mayst yenn (throw) a stone to Dame's, and mayst zee her every day.' Betty is delighted. 'I know every crick and cornder of et, by tale and by token.' What is more, Robin has already told her that his grandmother 'left me a pritty plat o' taty (potato) ground' and he owns an oak settle and a collection of household items. By allowing him to list these, Mary Palmer provides a useful insight into the sort of things a young country couple of limited means in the 18th century might gather together when setting up house: an iron porridge crock, a griddle, a brandis (three-legged trivet), a frying pan, a fender, some clome or earthenware dishes and some trenchers, a firkin and a trindle or big tub, some good knives and a big brass kettle that could be swapped for something else they might need. He also has a tester bed, pillows and pillow slips, a brand new pair of canvas sheets and another slightly worn pair.

For her part, Betty says she has forty shillings owed to her for wages, two silver apostle spoons, her mother's amber necklace and a ring. The clothes she owns 'will zarve for years, way a leet (little) patching,' and her aunt Madge has promised her a butt (hive) of bees. Her enthusiasm growing, she thinks of keeping a cow (Robin tells her that his father has promised a 'main good' one when they marry) and a pig, if she sells her spoons to pay for it. 'Then the milk I can 't zell, and the waste taties, and a leet draft and gruel, will be choice to pop en away and make en plim' (fat).

In the final dialogue they visit the house they hope to rent, once occupied by Gonmer Monford, a daughter of a former parson of the parish, who kept the school they both attended. ''Twas a good zoul. I lov'd her dearly,' Robin says. 'I ne'er pass her grave without halting. If I'de a cheeld I shou'd wish et to love me, as I lov'd her. I often think of the stories her used to tell; and of a zinshiny day her wid let es go out under the great tree, and her zit in the shade in the midst o' es.'

She had been a keen gardener, so much so that when her plants increased too much, she planted them out in a field 'and pricked out the toppings of rosen and jasmine in the hedges'. She had told Betty, 'If I'm bereaved o' my garden, I'm bereaved o' the comfort o' my life'. (Robin remarks, 'Her used to tell (talk) to her flowers', showing that talking to flowers is no new thing).

Betty imagines herself taking her knitting or her spinning wheel and sitting in the garden, 'and then I mert happen to zee thee, when you be to work. Dear heart! what strange things come to pass. When I used to think how happy any body mert live in such a sweet place, I could ne'er ha' thort it wid come to my take, everything so handy; a pretty cloming oven, big enew to take a batch o' bread, water at the shet (spring) just by, the thorn hedge, and garden, and the great tree.' Robin, too, foresees a happy future: ' . . . how comfortable 'twill be, arter es ha' been digging and delving all day, to be welcom'd home by thy sweet vace, to a chimly cornder (chimney corner) o' my own, and a house as clean as a pick.'

He asks again if he shall 'put in the banns next Zinday' and she assents. Yet even now, the malignity of John Hogg casts a shadow. She warns Robin to take care of himself and not to stay out late. He asks why. She answers, 'I han't a' be myzell since I've a inkling a' geed me, that Measter was gwain to get thee prest.'

This is a reminder that in the 18th century press gangs were still very active, seizing men for service at sea, as they had been since Tudor times (many of the men who fought for Armada had been pressed into the navy). An instance of the custom appears in 'The London Prodigal': when the Devon clothier Oliver first appears he is talking to some men who have been taken by a press gang commanded by Sir Arthur Greenfield, who tells him that his authority 'will stretch to press so good a man as you,' to Oliver's great indignation.

Although Robin knows that Hogg bears him a grudge for playing a trick on him, he makes light of the threat — but as they say goodnight and part, the reader is left wondering whether all their hopeful plans may come to nothing, and whether Robin may indeed 'go for a solger', though not voluntarily.

While the 'Exmoor Courtship' derived from the north-east corner of Devon, Mary Palmer's dialogues belong to the north-west. She makes it clear that Robin and Betty live somewhere near Torrington. At one point Robin describes trying to cross the frozen river Torridge because he saw Betty on the other side, and the cruelly ill-treated boy Bat, asked by Hogg in front of a group of onlookers, ''Ot did God make thee vor?' answers innocently, 'To carry dung to Crowbear'. A farm of that name still exists a few miles north-east of Torrington.

Growing up in Plympton, Mary Palmer would have become familiar with the dialect of south Devon, but it may not have differed greatly from the one she heard around Torrington. In general, her use of it is more restrained than that of the 'Exmoor Scolding's' author, though there are a few forceful passages, such as the one already quoted describing the two over-dressed women in church on Revel Sunday, and others in which Hogg makes some of his curmudgeonly speeches ('I'll ha' thee to know, thou make-bate, pick-thank hussy, that a man o' eight-and-twenty pounds a year, every voot his own land, and that pays vor everything 'pon the nail, may have, any day o' the week, a better servant than such a noizy, chuckling, make-strife as thee art') or Robin speaks of his hatred for the farmer ('The gluttish gorbelly pig. I wish somebody wul mawl he soundly. I wish I'de the trimming o' en, the slouching lubber, odds danget, I'd lerrick en to the true ben'.)

One difference is striking: although Mary Palmer was writing only some twenty years after Andrew Brice first brought out the 'Scolding', she never makes use of 'ch' in place of 'I'; her characters never say 'chell', 'chid' and so on.

While the Exmoor dialogues may be more earthy, Mary Palmer's give a more rounded view of contemporary rural life, even though it appears somewhat idealised. The Revel with its wrestling, dancing and jollification, the misery of very young pauper children if they happened to be apprenticed to a brutish master, the much happier lives of children with stable homes attending a well-run village school, the threat of the press gang, the way in which a young couple might scrape together the things they needed to set up house — all these combine to make the work an interesting fragment of social history as well as an example of mid-18th century Devon dialect.

Chapter Three

18th/19th Century: four writers of popular dialect verse

As a Devon-born cleric wrote a satirical account of Charles I's visit to Plymouth in dialect verse, so a Devon-born cleric, John Wolcot, wrote a satirical account of George III's visit to Exeter in 1789 in dialect verse. In both cases the work seems to have been the only example of its author writing in his native dialect.

Wolcot (1738-1819) became widely known under a pseudonym, Peter Pindar.[1] Born at Dodbrooke and educated at schools at Liskeard and Bodmin, he was apprenticed to his uncle, an apothecary-surgeon in Fowey. Although he was sent to London when he was twenty-four to continue medical studies, his diploma as doctor of medicine was granted by Aberdeen University. The following year, 1768, he went out to Jamaica as physician to the household of the governor, Sir William Trelawney, who offered him a change of profession: he could become rector of a parish on the island if he took holy orders. (Did Sir William have cause to doubt Wolcot's medical skills?) Returning promptly to London, Wolcot managed to get himself ordained in the remarkably casual fashion of those days, only to find that the living he had expected in Jamaica was not available. However, he was presented to another. On the death of Trelawney in 1772 he accompanied Lady Trelawney to England. He had dedicated a volume of verse with the title *Persian Love Elegies* to her.

Reverting to medicine he practised in Truro in what seems to have been a somewhat eccentric manner for several years, but in 1779 moved to London, where he spent the rest of his life. He had discovered the artistic talent of John Opie, the son of a Cornish mine carpenter, and helped to launch the young man as a successful society portrait painter — even the king bought two paintings.

Wolcot soon began to acquire a reputation as a writer of satirical verse. He first used the name Peter Pindar when he brought out, at his own expense, a collection, *Lyric Odes to the Royal Academicians for 1782.* Later his work was taken over by a publisher. Immensely prolific (one edition of his collected works runs to five volumes) he became one of the best known figures in the literary life of his time. His friend Thomas Giddy observed that 'the keenness of his satire and the novelty of his sentiments together with the peculiarity of his versification, made his productions exceedingly popular and they were bought with great avidity.'

Wolcot's savage satires on various members of the aristocracy might well have made him the subject of litigation, but somehow he was never brought to court. He repeatedly ridiculed George III, yet for many years the afflicted monarch accepted his attacks good-humouredly.

In August, 1789, the king was recovering from the first of his intermittent bouts of madness. With the Queen and their three daughters, he went to his favourite watering place, Weymouth, bathed in the sea, strolled on the sands, and evidently benefited from the change of scene. After a few days the royal party moved on to Exeter, 'the ever faithful city', which had celebrated the king's recovery with gunfire and illuminations. Travelling by way of Axminster (where they visited a carpet factory), Bridport and Charmouth, greeted everywhere by cheering crowds, they arrived at Exeter on the evening of August 13th. At the bounds of the city they were welcomed by the mayor and corporation, 'with an excellent band of music'. The mayor presented the keys of the city, 'which His Majesty politely returned saying, "They are already in very good hands."' An 'elegant supper' was provided at the Deanery. The next day the mayor and corporation attended the king with an address, and the royal family visited the cathedral, looking at 'everything curious or interesting that was to be seen, and then returned to dine at the Dean's. In the memory of man, there never was seen so great a concourse of people as were assembled from all parts of the adjacent country on this occasion.'

On August 15th the king and his family set off for Plymouth, reaching Saltram in the afternoon.

These details appear in an account of the tour which was published in journal form in the issues of the 'Gentleman's Magazine' for October, November and December, 1780.

Wolcot's description of the visit did not appear until 1795; it was included in a four volume edition of his collected works, brought out in London between 1794 and 1796 (two previous collections had been published in Dublin). It runs to fifty-nine six-line stanzas and is in the form of a letter from 'Brether Jan' to 'Zester Nan' and as has been said, is the only known example of Wolcot's use of dialect. Its anti-royalist tone is milder than Strode's: for the most part Wolcot simply seems to enjoy mocking the more absurd aspects of the reception of a monarch by a provincial city.

There is of course the eagerness of the ordinary people to see the king and his family:

'Now meend me, Nan! all Exeter town
Was gapin, rennin up and down,
Vath, just leek vokes bewitch'd!
Lord! how they lang'd to see the King;
To hear un zay zom marv'llous thing!
Leek mangy dogs they itch'd.'

and

'Vull as an egg was all the Church,
Vor vokes were mad as hares in March!

And fath it was dam quare,
To see ould Dames wey leathern chacks,
Hoisted upon the fellow's backs —
A penny for a stare.'

There is Squire Rolle,
'Close by the King's coach trotting,
Now shovin in the coach his head,
Meaning, we giss'd, it might be zed,
"The Squire and the King be chattin".'

There is the question of a speech of thanks to the king for his visit,

but when Squire Rolle points this out to the mayor and aldermen, they are dismayed:

'Why we be only men in trade;
'Tis true a vieow good pounds we've made —
Be tolerably rich:
But thoff we've raked up zom vieow pence,
It doth not vollow we've the sense
To make the King a speech.'

(The solution is to send for the Recorder, and commission him to write a speech 'That zimm'd to pleaze King George's taste')

Squire Rolle takes it upon himself 'To git the names of ev'ry soul,

That wish'd King George to zee', and marshals them into the king's presence:

'And vath no woundy fuss was made
'Bout dress amongst the men in trade,
They thort o' no zich thing;
Wey derty sharts and grisly beards,
Much leek a greazy pack o' keards,
They shuffled vore the King.;

Wolcot's portrayal of king himself is less harsh than in some of his other satires. He admires the way in which he 'stude patient as a stone, Vour hours at least by Exter (sic) clock', and calls him a jolly gentleman. However, he does find a good deal to criticise. The king did not move about the city to visit such places as the Guildhalll and the Castle, and so allow himself to be seen by the crowds. He did not attend a banquet prepared in his honour by the mayor. He promised to give something to the hospital, but did not do so.

Wolcot's John Ploughshare, 'a farmer of Morton-Hampstead', to whom the verses are attributed, ends on a dismissive note:

'Theeze once I've made my zelf a vool,
And now I feel my courage cool
For zeeing Royal Things:
And when my Bible next I rede,
Zo leet (little) I worship all the breed,
I'll skip the book of Kings.'

It seems possible that Henry Baird, a young man working in a solicitor's office in Exeter in the 1840s, had read Wolcot's work.[2] He began to write a series of dialect letters in verse. Like Wolcot, he adopted a pen name: when his efforts began to appear in local newspapers — the 'Western Times' in particular — he called himself Nathan Hogg. In 1847 a London publisher, J. Russell Smith, brought out a collection, *Nathan Hogg's Letters to es Brither* (not Brether, as in Wolcot) *Jan'*. They attracted a good deal of attention, and went into five editions. Local reviews were favourable. The 'Western Times' considered that the author's extensive knowledge of the Devonshire dialect was very ingenious as well as picturesque. The 'Exeter Flying Post' remarked that 'those who know anything of the social characteristics of the rural populations of the County, will recognise the fidelity and ability with which the Author has depicted them'. The 'Plymouth Mail', observing that the letters had achieved considerable popularity, thought that the 'continuous flow of wit and humour throughout, cannot fail to operate forcibly upon the risible faculties of the reader.'

Baird was able to leave his poorly-paid clerking job and join the staff of the 'Plymouth Mail'. After a year or two he returned to work on the 'Western Times', and later became a bookseller in St Martin's Lane, Exeter, but was not very successful. Eventually he moved to London; a news agency appointed him their Old Bailey reporter. However, he was in failing health, and died at the age of about fifty-two.[3]

The first letter to 'Brither Jan', 'Tha Hossmanship' (The Horsemanship) is dated April 12th, 1846. By adopting the persona of the wide-eyed countryman at large in the city, (as Strode had done two centuries earlier) Baird was able to cast a mildly satirical eye on local happenings. The equestrian displays in 'Tha Hossmanship' were apparently made by some kind of travelling circus troupe; another, a month later, 'Tha Wile Baistes' brought an elephant, a rhinoceros, monkeys, a pelican and a woman lion tamer. Nathan marvels at a hot air balloon, and reflects that

'If Vather and old Hunkel Will cude bit zee
Tha things thit be dooing, how vrighten'd they'd be!'

He travels on the South Devon Railway between Exeter and Teignmouth on its opening day in June, 1846. He visits fairs; at one he has his pocket picked by 'a purty gal, bit a chaiting yung thing', and at another finds that the rifle in the shooting gallery won't shoot straight. Baird uses Nathan to make some social comment: watching the extravagance of a fancy dress ball ('Bout tha Vancy Bal') he says

'Dear Jan how more nauble twid be ta be shore,
If they's gie haf tha munny they waste ta tha pore',

and at one of the fairs he notes that policemen harass working people but

'Tu a veller drest wul they niver zes nort
An that are's tha rais'n a new coat I've bort.'

However, when bread riots break out in Exeter, and a crowd of women 'A ballin and kikkin up zich a ta doo' attack bakers' shops, he regards their poverty with scepticism:

'An I'm zartin, dear brither, as miny ulse thort,
Thit haf awmin dude et wat didd'n want nort.'

As a result, he is 'Zwared in as a kunstabil zarving tha Queen.'

This letter is dated May, 1847. The riots described began when a mob of women 'and idlers' attacked a man for 'forestalling' — that is to say buying up the potato supply before it reached the market. Special Constables were hastily sworn in and the military called out. (Similar riots occurred ten years later, when 'The Crimean War and the cruel January weather combined to push food prices up to a level which caused considerable hardship to the poor . . . bakers' shops were attacked . . . the Mayor called out the 3rd Light Dragoons . . . the presence of the cavalry and the enrolment of a large number of special constables quenched the unrest.')[4]

At a performance of amateur theatricals by 'The Gentlemen Ackters', Nathan affects to be shocked by

. . . the Ladies' vine dresses and haids
Dude up vur ta make em aul luke purty maids;
Bit one thing I almost vurgot tu a named —
Thare necks and thare buzzims most made mer ashamed.'

There is one mention of a national event, when Nathan draws his brother's attention to an item in the 'Exeter Gazette', 'Jan Moody's Letter pin the Crimyin War', dated 8th October, 1856. Jan, a 'labering chap', claims to know about 'tha war that's gwain on' (he asks if it's true that the Russians boil down English and French soldiers to make candles: evidently atrocity stories were rife). By the time 'Jan Moody' was writing, the Crimean War had been ended by the Treaty of Paris in the previous month; Baird was apparently making fun of the countryman's limited knowledge of events.

The collection ends with a long verse narrative running to some 800 lines. 'Tha old Humman way the Urd Cloke, a Witch Story'. (Baird consistently uses 'urd' for red, as here, 'urch' for rich, 'burches' for breeches, 'urn' for run and even 'pirnt' for print. This metathesis seems to have been in more frequent use in some parts of Devon than others.)

In a lengthy note he said that 'Paragraphs may frequently be seen in the newspapers headed "Extraordinary Belief in Witchcraft", "Lamentable Case of Superstition!", etc. etc., and the readers thereof become duly astonished, throw up their hands, and ejaculate "Can such things be in the Nineteenth Century?" Verily such things can be and are . . . an afternoon's excursion now and then, into some of the villages and hamlets within a few miles of this ever faithful city, where, in many instances, the Railway is supposed to have borne intelligence, and the Electric Wire to have flashed enlightenment, and thou will find that the belief in Witchcraft and the appearance of Ghosts exists . . . and that, however "lamentable", superstitions of this kind are as general as is the vernacular in which the aforesaid story is written.'

With a few exceptions, the versified letters — and the witch story — are written in rhyming couplets, making for some tedium as the rhymes thump relentlessly along. Perhaps Baird became aware of this, as his second collection contains mainly poems of six, eight or even twelve-line stanzas, although two long ghost stories, 'Mucksy Lane' and 'Tha Kenton Gost' (sic) are again in rhyming couplets. Having abandoned the epistolary form, Baird divided this collection into what he called 'Sair-yiss Poams' and 'Humeriss Poams'. The serious ones include 'Tha Daisy tap tha Grave', in which the flower becomes a symbol of a child's spirit, and 'Twenty Yurs — a Raycollelckshin', 'Gwayn Hom' and 'Tha Zinging Time a Live', all in one way or another lamenting the changes brought by time. The humorous ones show Nathan making a speech at a council meeting, visiting a Turkish bath, and having his photograph taken and in 'A Turrable Ride be Rayl' he has a nightmare in which he travels on the *outside* of a train between Teignmouth and Exeter.

Baird devoted 63 six-line stanzas to 'Expairyances uv Roylty'. One shows Nathan accidentally finding himself in a first class carriage occupied by the young Prince Arthur and two attendants; in another he sees Queen Victoria at Saltram in 1854. A third proudly records meetings with Prince Louis Lucien Bonaparte, who visited Exeter and sought out Baird to talk about Devon dialect.

Prince Louis, born in 1813, was the third son of Napoleon's second surviving brother, and so a cousin of Napoleon III. Nevertheless he was born in Thorngrove, Worcestershire, spent his youth in Italy, and did not go to France until 1848. In that year he served a brief term in the Assembly as representative for Corsica, and the next year represented the Seine. Yet he was clearly more a scholar than a politician, and was perhaps happier in England than in France; he certainly devoted much time to studying English dialects, although he also published works in the Basque language.

Baird asked if he might dedicate his second verse collection to the prince. In granting permission, the latter said that 'as far as my humble individual opinion about your ability in the Devonshire Dialect, I can only say that all the most intricate and difficult questions about the pronunciations and other grammatical proprieties of this very interesting dialect have been answered by you in such a manner as to enable me to propose to you, and adopt with your approval, several of the modifications of orthography admitted for the Gospel of St Matthew, the which I certainly could never have attained except through a person thoroughly acquainted, as you, in my opinion, undoubtedly are, with the peculiarities of this curious form of the English speech'.

Baird reproduced this letter, and his own painfully obsequious dedicatory letter, in the book, which may have raised the hackles of readers old enough to remember the long years during which the prince's uncle had ravaged much of Europe.

'In seeking the honour which your Highness has so readily and courteously conferred upon me, by granting me permission to dedicate to you the following pages, I feel assured that you will better appreciate my object in doing so when I admit that, while entertaining full respect for your exalted rank, a recollection of the Prince becomes lost in my admiration for the Linguist.

Remembering the many interviews which I have been privileged to have with your Highness, during your study of the Devonshire Dialect, and your extraordinary mastery of its general peculiarities and most difficult idioms, I can well understand how highly you have deserved the honourable mention which has been made of you as a Linguist by the European Press.

My testimony to that already so universally given may seem to savour somewhat of egotism. I cannot however imagine that I have committed any great breach of modesty in seeking, as the humble student of one dialect, the appreciation of a perfect master of hundreds'.

Reading Baird's verse it becomes clear that of the three principal elements of a language or one of its dialects — grammar, vocabulary and pronunciation — it is pronunciation that interests him most. He provided an almost identical glossary, each of about 240 words, to his two books, but these contain few words from the rich vocabulary of rural Devon, such as are found in the 18th century dialogues and elsewhere; they merely provide the dictionary English forms of words in general use which he has rendered phonetically in dialect. Sometimes, as when he spells 'rail' as 'rayl', 'there' as 'thare', 'eight' as 'aight' and 'ghost' as 'gost', his alterations seem pointless, as do the renderings of words containing the sound ordinarily spelled 'ought' or 'aught' — nort, bort, thort, etc. He observed in a note that 'two of the greatest peculiarities in the Devonshire Dialect are the pronunciation of *a* and *u*, as in the Scotch gude and the English cat'. In accordance with this, he ensured that, throughout his Second Series, the letters *a* and u were italicised in all words containing the 'gude' and 'cat' sounds. That pronunciation was also Prince Louis's main interest is indicated by the reference, in his letter to Baird already quoted, to his attempt to produce a dialect version of St Matthew's gospel. In his 'Expairyances uv Roylty', Baird gleefully recorded that the prince had told him that he wanted to listen to

'Zich purty spaykin chaps ez you,
Ta put thare talk in pirnt' (sic)

and that if Nathan would

. . . turn tha Zing
Uv Zolamin into my tung
He'd pay me vur et wul.'

(Had the prince come across Defoe's account of the Martock schoolboy's rendering of a verse from that book?)

In view of this, it is somewhat surprising that Prince Louis commissioned another assiduous rhymester, George Pulman, to do the same thing. Pulman's west country 'Song of Solomon' was published by the English Dialect Society in 1860 in an edition of two hundred and fifty copies.

George Philip Rigney Pulman was born in Axminster in 1819. A talented amateur musician, he became organist of Axminster church at the age of twenty. During the next four years he published three books all in some way connected with his great interest, fishing. His *Vade-Mecum of Fly Fishing for Trout* was followed by *Rustic Sketches, being Rhymes and "Skits"* on *Angling and other Subjects* and *The Book of the Axe*. (This was the Devonshire river Axe, which gives its name to Axminster, not the Somerset river of the same name which flows into Weston Bay.) In 1848 he left Devon for Somerset, having acquired a printing and stationery business at Crewkerne — although for some years he continued as organist at Axminster, which would have entailed a journey of some twelve miles every weekend. He founded a newspaper called 'Pulman's Weekly News', priced at three-halfpence; he also published the 'Bridport News' and was for a time editor of the 'Yeovil Times'.[5]

Prefacing the third edition of the *Rustic Sketches*, in 1871, with 'Remarks on the West of England Dialects', he observed that 'The Devonshire man is detected in a moment. His first friendly greeting "How be yewe's moarning?" betrays him, and even the particular part of the county becomes revealed by intonation. One of the first of living linguists manifests his Devonshire origin in the utterance of half a dozen syllables . . . 'This is almost certainly a reference to Sir John Bowring, whom Pulman had met, as he must also have met Prince Louis Bonaparte.

He interspersed his dialect verses on the joys of angling with several prose pieces, all except one also concerned in some way with fishing. The exception is 'Job's Patience'.

'Poor wold Job Clarke com'd home one night wet dru to es very skin, an' went straight off to bed. Es wife Ratchell had a-bin baking in the day-time, and she put Job's lethern burches (breeches) into the open (sic) to dry'em. In th' morning, avore 'twas light, Job began to veel about vor es things, an' miss'd th' burches, "Where be my burches?" zes he, " — where *be* my burches, Ratchell?" "Well, bless my zoul," zes she, "if I han't a-left 'em in the open!" Away goes Job aader 'em, but in a minnit zings out, "Massy wull, what in the wordle (sic) hev ee done, Ratchell? They be all cockled up lik a skin o' parchment! O, Lor', O, Lor'! What shall I do? Was ever a feller plagued zo avore?" "Paatience, Job, paatience," zes th' wold body, "hev a little paatience. Remember your namesake, how he was caddled."

"Aye, aye, that's vurry true," zes Job. "He had a nation zight to put up wi', that's zartin', but ez wive neer baked es burches."'

A third writer who was publishing west country dialect verse around the middle of the 19th century was H.J. Daniel (1818-1889). He was a Cornishman, born at Lostwithiel. Unlike Baird and Pulman, he did not need to earn his own living. His father, a grocer — evidently a very successful one — died when he was only sixteen, leaving him enough money to keep him in comfort for life. He is said to have written 'about a thousand short poetical pieces.' He published many of them, presumably at his own expense, in a series of sixpenny paperback booklets, each containing between ten and twenty verse narratives with such titles as 'The Muse in Motley', 'Mirth for long Evenings', ' Wit and Humour, or Fun and Frolic'.

Although much of his writing was concerned with his native county, one of his booklets contains 'Roger and Patty, an eclogue in the Devonshire Dialect'. Like the 'Exmoor Courtship', or Mary Palmer's or William Rock's pieces, it is a courtship dialogue, but it is shorter than its predecessors, running to only about 150 lines.

Roger and Patty meet somewhere out of doors on the first of May. He asks her to sit down on a tree root ('A plummer zait thee cussent vind, I'm zure') and offers her basam (heather) and 'happle blooth' (apple blossom). He wastes no time in telling her of his feelings:

'Sitch ees, sitch vace, sitch huxens (ankles) and sitch leps (lips)

Your huxens, Patty, clainer than new pins

Vraped in whit stockings, plague me vor my zins'.

Patty responds briskly, 'Co, no blind mares' (nonsense), and accuses him of saying the same sort of things to other girls; only the previous Sunday she heard he was with Lizzie Jeele, a 'colting maid'.

Indignantly he denies this, and tells her he'll hang or drown himself, or take poison ('gulk a pound o' pison in my brath') if she won't marry him. He turns to practicalities:

'I got a little stub (sum) o' money, cheeld,

And mains to buy a cow, an' kip a field;

An' to the puggen-end (gable end) o' our house
Vraith (wattle) up a vitty linhay vor the cows;
An' in the garden, orts (dung) I'll ev in heaps
An' taty-inyins-grow in lammin greeps (great bunches).
No deberries (gooseberries) vor size shall aiquel mine;
Patty, my dear, we'll faggee well a fine'. (do well in the end).

Although Patty says she doesn't believe a quarter of what he says, if he'll take his 'affidavy' to marry her, she'll give notice to leave her job.

The delighted Roger exclaims 'Ods, wunderakins! bless your pretty vace', and imagines the rejoicing at their wedding. The piece ends limply as they part, promising to meet again the next evening; the energy and drama of similar dialogues is lacking.

Daniel had his booklets published in Devonport and London, and claimed that they were 'Sold by all Booksellers and at the Railway Bookstalls' — as Elworthy had remarked that an edition of the 'Exmoor Courtship and Scolding' 'may now be bought at the Railway Bookstalls, apparently reprinted from the edition of 1771, with the preface and vocabulary, price sixpence.' While it is not surprising that the increasing popularity of rail travel in mid-Victorian times had justified the setting up of bookstalls at stations, it is more unexpected to find evidence that they thought it worth their while to stock books in Devon dialect.

Chapter Four

Mid-19th Century: William Rock's 'Jim and Nell' and a letter to a sister

The title page of a little book published in London in 1867 reads 'Jim and Nell, a dramatic poem in the dialect of North Devon by a Devonshire Man. Printed for private circulation.'

The Devonshire man was William Frederick Rock, a Barnstaple-born businessman who spent the greater part of his life in London. Like Baird and Pulman, he had a fondness for writing verse, but 'Jim and Nell' seems to be the only example of his doing so in dialect. He was born in 1802, the son of a shoemaker who was of sufficient standing to become a freeman of the borough and thus one of the limited group of voters at parliamentary elections. A political friend secured for his son a presentation to Christ's Hospital, the London Bluecoat School. Having received a sound education, the young William came back to Barnstaple and accepted the offer of a job in a bank in Bideford. A habit of writing verse in office hours apparently earned him a reprimand; he promptly resigned and went to London, where a banker who had stood unsuccessfully for election in Barnstaple offered him a job. Later, Rock joined the firm of the printer-inventor, Thomas de la Rue; they made a modest fortune out of one of de la Rue's patents, embossed paper bonnets. Rock used his share to set up in business on his own in 1833, printing 'fancy and general stationery'. He took his brothers and his future brother-in-law into partnership, worked hard and prospered.

He retained a great affection for his native town, and visited it often. Although he never married, this kindly and generous man liked to speak of the people of Barnstaple as his children, and enjoyed thinking of ways in which he might use his fortune to help them. Apart from many private acts of generosity to individuals, he provided premises and money to make possible the setting up of a Literary and Scientific Institute in 1845. Four decades later, when the Institute seemed to have outgrown its usefulness, he bought a large house in the Square, endowed it with the then very large sum of £12,000, and presented it to the town: in 1888 it was opened as the North Devon Athenaeum. One other major gift was the open area beside the river Taw, developed as a pleasure ground and still known as Rock Park.

In the words of a Barnstaple friend, 'over a period of more than forty years, he continued to throw off a vast amount of fugitive poetry and literature', but 'Jim and Nell' is perhaps his most interesting and individual work. His declared aim was 'to interweave every provincial word known to the Author . . . few verses have been added . . . without the introduction of at least three or four new words. This may have, in many instances, interfered with the poetical interest of the tale, but will, it is presumed, increase its local value. The Author is not aware of any composition formed on a similar plan, and he must reiterate that the object of the story of Jim and Nell is to string together, not merely the county pronunciation, but the idioms and the provincialisms of the Devonshire dialect.' He added a glossary of some 800 words.

There are three parts or, as Rock spells it, 'pearts'. The setting of part one is 'Guenever Varm'. After fussing around making sure that the servants have everything ready, the farmer's wife welcomes the neighbours to a meal.

'Cum. neybors, doo dra nigh tha board,
Tha very best us can avoord —
Cum, all know where vor zit.'

She offers them squab pie (a favourite Devon dish of apples, onions and mutton), goose, the edible seaweed laver, spring onions, roast veal, mugget pie (muggets or mugguts were the intestines of animals), doucet pie (a sweet herb pie), apple dumplings and cream, and whitpot, a mixture of flour, milk and treacle.

Afterwards Jan Scrape the Crowder (fiddler) plays for dancing, and later the young ones play a sort of hide and seek.

Finally the hostess gives her blessing to the engagement of Jim Barrow and Nelly Brown, and asks Jim's employer, 'Varmer Voord', to agree to the match. He answers:

'Wi' all ma hert. Ees, Jim and Nell
'E've zarved yer Dame an' maisters well,
And yer rayward shall vend;
I'll gie the 'ouse, hoy, an' hadge round',
Smaal-acker Close vor gurden groun',
An' proud to caal th'a vrend . . .

Thee's din thee dooty all thee live
Now do thee dooty to thee wive —
Nelly gie Jim thee hand . . .

An' thees day month, if all be well,
Our Jim, please God, 'll marry Nell —
All meet ta Whitveel Barton'.

Part Two is the wedding day, and the presents brought by each guest are reported: all kinds of things a young country couple setting up house would find useful, beginning with a four-poster bed with 'vittings prapper' and a variety of kitchen utensils, including a skillet, keigers (casks), a trindle (salting tub) and even a lantern. Perhaps more important, as Jim and Nell are evidently expected to be running their own smallholding at Small Acre

Close, are agricultural implements: harness for a draught horse, a pair of crooks (a sort of wooden yoke for use on a packhorse), a dredge or bush harrow and a velling plough, used for taking off turf. Most valuable of all are a 'prime yaffer' (heifer) and two young sows.

No fewer than 24 maidens arrive as attendants on the young couple when they go to church. Nell returns blushing but happy, and Farmer Ford makes a speech ending with the traditional wish, 'be all zingle married zoon, And all tha marri'd happy' before the whole party moves off to Barracott for a wedding feast.

When the third part, headed 'Scene out ta Barracott', begins, almost fifteen years have passed; Jim reflects gloomily on neighbours and friends who have died during that time, beginning with 'Varmer Voord, an' Dame' and going on to mention a dozen or so others who have been killed in accidents or fights or died as the result of eating or drinking something harmful, including 'pixy-stools'.

Nell tires of this and begins to talk about their two young sons. Presently the boys come in with 'rabbits'-mait' — food for their pet rabbits. They say they have found the nests of a 'corniwill' (lapwing), a copperfinch' (chaffinch) and a hoop (bullfinch). Nell tells the younger boy to stay in while she mends his breeches, and the elder to go to look for angletwitches, cubabys, maskells and oakems (worms, ladybirds, caterpillars and cockchafers) to feed the fledglings — an impractical and improbable idea to come from a countrywoman. When the boys have had their supper and gone to bed, the couple congratulate one another on their children and the happiness of their marriage. The final verses express Jim's definition of married love:

'. . . But when a heart weds way a heart,
When soul weds soul they'll never part
Vor this is heavenly marri'ge.

An surely, Nell, zich luv is ours,
An' zo we'll pass our earthly hours,
While we together dwell;

That when in tha bright ways above,
Two spirits fly still joined in love,
They'll zay "That's Jim and Nell"'

There is a certain irony in the fact that this idealised view of happy marriage was written by a lifelong bachelor.

'Jim and Nell' consists of 137 six-line rhymed stanzas. If Rock had indeed done little more than string together words and idioms, as he claimed, the result might have been barely readable, virtually a versified glossary. In fact he showed considerable skill and ingenuity in employing his chosen verse form to tell his simple tale without seeming to force either the dialect words or their meaning into the lines. Although his glossary runs to about 800 words, twenty or thirty of these are words to be found in ordinary English dictionaries; for instance, gaff, heft, horseplay, lissom, mallard, nudge, pudgy, slapdash, swathe, trivet and so on.

For the most part, the tone is genial, and Rock allowed Farmer Ford to display the sort of generosity that was his own admirable characteristic in providing Jim and Nell with a house and some land. At the same time, like earlier writers in dialect, he evidently wanted to show his command of the sort of vigorous language which his fellow Devonians might use to disparage others. In Part Two Grace Gray, a friend of Nell who works at 'Whitveel Barton', confesses to her mistress that she is in love with a man who at one time paid her a lot of attention but is now attracted to another girl. Dame has no use for the man. Rock devotes six stanzas to her vehement criticism of him. He is a 'bibbling, boostering, brinded chap. A dunderhead hadge-boar' and both a 'lubbercock gurt wangery toad' and a 'tilty, twily, preckett toad'; also a 'panking. puffing nestledraff', a 'quirking fule' and a poor workman ('A niver carr'th but half a load'). In other words, she considers him a bibulous, flustering, sour-looking chap, a stupid hedgehog, a testy, troublesome, conceited toad, a turkeycock who is also a great flabby toad, a panting, feeble runt, a grumbling fool, and a workman who never carries more than half a load. Finally she assures Grace that she is of 'too good haveage' (breeding or background) for him. Grace merely answers that she is 'dunch' (deaf) to all this and loves the man 'as my loive'.

Whereas Baird, Pulman and Rock probably had publication is mind from the beginning, others may have been content to write in dialect only for their own amusement, or for that of their friends, as Mary Palmer evidently did. The volume of the Devonshire Association's Transactions for 1913 included a dialect letter which R.P. Chope, who submitted it, called 'an interesting and valuable specimen of Devonshire dialect of fifty or sixty years ago', which would mean that it was written not long after the delayed publication of Mary Palmer's dialogues, and Baird and Pulman's books had appeared. He said that it had been 'composed by a lady resident in the South of Devon, and much accustomed to the poor people's dialect.' He pointed out that it was intended 'not as an imitation of a letter *written* by a peasant, but rather to show how such a person would *talk*.'

'I take this yer opportunity to zen' to 'e, an' tell 'e about me an' Tom gwain auver to zee Oncle. Tom was in zich hurry to zet voar that he was spuddlin' avaur vive o'clock. Us zet away purty airly. I'd a-got up my best shoes, an' Tom he was up in his best hat. Mary would ha' putt us gwain, but down home, where it lieth lew, 't had a-been deevin', an' her thort her'd be voagin' o' mux till her was gerried up to huxons, zo her bide home. When us com'd up a tap o' the clapper. 't was all a-vraur up, an' the pillum blaw'd right in our faces. Us went along purty good coo'se, on'ny Tom's always bad in his knee and' fetch'th his-zel in gwain, zo that hiner'd us a bit. When we com'd to Oncle's, Aunt told us her'd been puttin' out eye vor us siverl days. Oncle was to baid in his voot, and' hadn't been down auver stairs zince Zinday was wick, but he was better an' caal'd down to us to com up in chimber. He'd hain'd up his haid an' zot up on eend the baid. He ax'd us to putch, an' us zat tellin' most pairt o'hour. He'd a-putt cow-flop leaves to a' voot, an' that's most principlest thing for the infurmation. He was bad, sure 'nuff, last wick, hadn't a-got no stummick to a' mait, an' didn't ait nat the vally o' a mail's mait, an Aunt tried all but iv'rything; her thort he'd be a parfit natomy, but the doctor gie'd zom trade to crave un to appetite, zo las' Thursday Aunt kill'd the young stag and strub un', an' I help swail'd un' an' her boiled up a few broth, an' Oncle let down two or dree o'n. When us com'd down vrom chimber, us went auver to the Blue Anchor arter zom plummin' vor Aunt. I catch'ed the skirt o' my coat in the hapse o' the geat, an' brauk'd out piece o' un; 't was much I hadn a-tor'd un all abroad. Aunt gie'd us a glorious dinner; her gearn's fairly a-dring'd up wi' salary, an' I love't dearly, but her zaid there was a sight o'volk bad about, an't us shouldn't ait no runch; her gie'd us bootivul apple-mait tho' an' us ait till us was quaat. Her toald us be sure and ait plenty o' dinner, vor fear us should be leary avaur us got home. Us was very comfor'ble, sure 'nuff, and niver thort how long us 'd a-stapt, 'vaur us yerd the clock strick vower. "Massy li, Tom!" says I, "'tis vower o'clock." "Soce," zays he, "you don't zay zo!" "'Tis tho'," says I, "an' Mother'll be in a fine vling, an' her'll gie't to us if us be late; vor her an' Mary was comin' agin us. Us mus' rin vor't." Oncle and Aunt toald us to mind they to all our volks, an' us cut away home, zo vast as us could lay legs to groun'. About a mile vrom Oncle's, ther'd been a bit o' a ruzement, and two trees, or zay dree then, was lie'd along the road, but us got auver 'em purty suant. "I'll wadge, Tom." says I, "'us shall be gwain a-thurt the groot-veel' in the dimmet." An' zo us was, an' when us com'd down auver the clapper, the moon was shinin' a tap o' the hailin' o' Father's barn. Mother and Mary was com agin us, an' was lookin' vor us back, an' I thort sure Mother would ha' discoos'd us auver vor bein' wantin' zo long, but her didn't zay nort about it.

Mind me to brither shoemaker. I'll waarn he'll wish he'd a-been 'long wi' us. Mary saith her's fairly got the flickets up to see my bad writin', but my hands be all a-scrim'd up wi' coald, an' bezides I've a-got chilpots 'pon 'em. Our roses be all a-davered; I reckon 'tis wi' the vraust. The cockabels be hangin' to the shillin' stones. I vorgot to zay that Cousin Bill's been bad in's vinger; he was swell'd up zo hard you mid zo well ha' tried to brit a stone. Mother zaith 'twas apse, eithermore a nimpingang; he zaith he squatt un. It made un look cruel bad.

I'm thinkin' you and Jack mid zo well ha' a bit o' a spree, an' com auver to our house wance vor the wick. If you com purty airly, you can stap a good bit an' be home again avaur candle-teenin'. I s'pose you've got a-mind in our young zow, I main he that was varried that time when poor ol' Gramfer lie'd by the wall — us kill'd las' Monday, an' Mother and Mary've made a fine lot of pot an' pudd'n. Father was on wi' 'em that they was boilin' o' 'm too long an' they'd be all zimzawed, but they bain't. The hin what you gie'd ma hath a-got nist up 'n the hay-tallet; he's zo fat 's a peg, an' 't veather' o'n be zo plum's a waant, but I zim he'll be broody avaur long.

Ol' Becky lieth jist in wan way. Her's a wisht poor blid, an' the doctor zaith her's very dangerous. Her 'th a-got the flusy faiver, but her hath'n nivver be to her-zel zince her poor ol' man died o' the narro-staples, or the standry's-vire. or 'siplis. or 'ot they caal 't. I'm afeared our Betsy's got no shakes o' a place; her missis is oncommon widdy-waddy zoart o' 'oman, an' zo itemin' there's no plaizin' her. Her's purty near too. Mother wish'th vor Betsy to stap out the winter if her can, any way, 'cause her zaith, havin' zich zight o' maidens home pick'th away a good bit o' money. Our young Squire stap'th in zometimes, an' hang'th up his mully in the linny, an't then I go an' clap 'n in the stable an' gie 'n a yafful o' wuts, zo t'other day mornin' he gie'd me scute, an' if you com I wish vor 'ee to bring ma handkercher like that there wan your Peggy's a-got. Mother's very naish an' git'th coald in her niddick 'pon times, an' I think a handkercher would hinder't.

Us zeed Farmer Dick go 'long las' Zinday up in all 's bais'ly clothes; 'twas quite onstummickable. Aunt Sally zaith her knaw'd they'd come to ruin, his missis was zich uncommon 'oman to bring things gwain, an' he wadn't nivver the wan to gie her riggin' vor't. Aunt zaith, her mind'th wan time they ax'd she and the maidens down to tay; 'twas summer time, an't they gie'd 'em yaws milk craim, an' that's the richest o' craims, but 'twadn't good 'nuff vor Missus, sure, an' her must have saft sugar 'pon 't. Aunt zaid her'd turn the stone, and nivver go there no more, vor her wouldn't let her maidens zee no zich doin's.

Aunt 'th a-zend word that Oncle's a power better; he croak'd out about in th' apple-gearn yis-day, an' look'th up more pearter 'n what he did, but he's walsh, poor man, now, an' no like to be no ither, jist vor prisint. He com'd down and zot in the parlour, where 'tis plaunchen vloor, las' wick.

Tom was bad in 's jaws las' night; he walk'd vo'th an' back, an't to an' agin tha chimber till he was jist rampin'. He'th jist had his tooth draw'd; there was zich maurs to 'n you'd be bless'd to zee 't. The doctor gie'd 'n two twicks, an' bullyragged Tom 'cause he scritch'd. He zaid he hadn't a-got no more heart 'n a goose-chick.'

In conventional English, this might be read as:

'I take this opportunity to send to you, and tell you about Tom and I going over to see Uncle. Tom was in such a hurry to get off that he was up and about before five o'clock. We set off pretty early. I was wearing my best shoes and Tom was in his best hat. Mary would have seen us on our way, but down there where we live, where it's sheltered; it had been thawing and she thought she'd be trudging in mud till she was plastered up to her ankles, so she stayed home. When we came to the top of the hill it was all frozen up, and the dust blew right in our faces. We went along at a pretty good rate only Tom's knee is bad, and he's a bit lame, so that hindered us a bit. When we arrived at Uncle's, Aunt told us she'd been looking out for us for several days. Uncle was in bed with his bad foot, and hadn't been downstairs since a week ago on Sunday, but he was better and called down to us to come up to the bedroom. He wrapped up his head and sat up in bed. He asked us to sit down and we sat talking for nearly an hour. He'd put foxglove leaves on his foot, and that's the best thing for inflammation. He was bad, sure enough, last week, and hadn't any appetite,, and hardly ate any food, and Aunt tried nearly everything; she thought he'd be an absolute skeleton, but the doctor gave him some stuff to give him an appetite, so last Thursday Aunt killed the young cockerel and plucked it, and I helped singe it, and she boiled up a little broth, and Uncle drank two or three helpings. When we came down from the bedroom we went over to the Blue Anchor to fetch some yeast for Aunt. I caught the skirt of my coat in the latch of the gate, and tore out a piece; it was a good thing I didn't rip it more. Aunt gave us a glorious dinner; her garden is fairly crowded with celery and I love it dearly, but she said that there were a lot of people ill round here, and we shouldn't eat any green stuff; she gave us some beautiful apples though, and we sate until we were full. She told us to be sure to eat plenty of dinner, for fear we should be hungry before we got home. We were certainly very comfortable, and never thought how long we'd stayed, until we heard the clock strike four. "Mercy on us, Tom," says I, "it's four o'clock." "Soce," says he, "you don't say so!"

"It is though," says I, "and Mother'll be in a fine state, and she'll give it to us if we're late — she and Mary were going to come to meet us. We must run for it." Uncle and Aunt told us to remember them to all our folks, and we cut away home as fast as we could put foot to ground. About a mile from Uncle's there'd been a bit of subsidence, and two trees, or perhaps three, were lying along the road, but we got over them pretty easily. "I bet, Tom," says I, "we'll be going across the ploughed field in the dusk." And so we were, and when we came down over the hill the moon was shining on the slates of Father's barn. Mother and Mary were coming to meet us, and I thought Mother would surely scold us for being away so long, but she didn't say anything about it.

Remember me to brother shoemaker. I bet he'll wish he'd been with us. Mary says she fairly blushes to see my bad writing, by my hands are all cramped with cold, and besides I've got chilblains on them. Our roses are all withered; I reckon it's the frost. Icicles are hanging on the eaves. I forgot to say Cousin Bill's had a bad finger; it was swelled up so hard you might as well have tried to dent a stone. Mother said it was an abscess, either that or a whitlow; he says he squashed it. It made him look very bad.

I'm thinking you and Jack might as well have a bit of a spree, and come over to our house one day in the week. If you come pretty early, you can stay a good bit and be home before candle-lighting time. I suppose you remember our young sow, the one that was born that time when poor old Granfer was dying — we killed it last Monday, and Mother and Mary have made a fine lot of hog's puddings. Father was telling them that they were boiling them too long, and they'd be overdone, but they aren't. The hen you gave me has got a nest up in the hay loft; she's as fat as a pig, and her feathers are as soft as moleskin, but I think she'll be broody before long. (The reference to both the sow and the hen as 'he' is in accordance with the long-standing tradition in Devon that made animals of either sex male.)

Old Becky is very ill. She's a poorly old soul, and the doctor says her condition is dangerous. She's got 'flu, but she's never been her old self since her poor old man died of St Anthony's Fire, or erysipelas, or whatever they call it. I'm afraid our Betty's place is no great shakes; her mistress is an uncommonly changeable sort of woman, and so fussy there's no pleasing her. She's pretty mean, too. Mother wants Betsy to stay there for the winter if she can, anyway, because she says having so many girls at home costs a good bit. Our young squire calls in sometimes, and leaves his donkey in the linhay, and then I go and put it in the stable and give it a handful of oats, so the other morning he gave me a tip, and if you come I wish you'd bring a scarf like the one your Peggy has got. Mother's very delicate, and gets a cold in her neck sometimes, and I think a scarf would prevent it.

We saw Farmer Dick go along last Sunday in all his scruffy clothes; it was disgusting. Aunt Sally say she knew they'd come to ruin; his missus was such a woman for extravagance, and he was never the one to scold her for it. Aunt says she remembers one time they asked her and her daughters down to tea; it was summer time and they gave them ewe's milk cream, and that's the richest of creams, but it wasn't good enough for Missus — she had to have soft sugar on it. Aunt said she'd resolved never to go there again, because she wouldn't let her girls see such things.

Aunt has sent word that Uncle's a lot better; he crept about in the apple garden yesterday, and looks brighter than he did, but he's weak, poor man, now, and not likely to be anything else for the moment. He came down and sat in the parlour, where there's a wooden floor, last week.

Tom had a pain in his jaw last night; he walked up and down the bedroom until he was just beside himself with pain. He's just had his tooth out; it had such a root you'd be blessed to see it. The doctor gave it two pulls, and told Tom off because he yelled. He says he hadn't got any more courage than a gosling.'

Chapter Five

Late 19th century: Sarah Hewett and 'The Peasant Speech of Devon'

In 1861 the remarkable Victorian geologist, William Pengelly, son of a Cornish seaman, was walking along Millbay Road in Plymouth with two friends. They were on their way to investigate a quarry behind St George's Hall, Stonehouse. Pengelly suddenly said, "I say, you men, I have been thinking lately that it would be a good idea if an Association for the county of Devon, on the lines of the British Association, could be formed." His companions were rather startled by the boldness of the idea, but agreed that it should 'have their warmest support if it were found to be practicable'. Later they expressed some doubts, but Pengelly persevered, and at a preliminary meeting in Plymouth in April, 1862, with ten men present, his proposition was carried unanimously, and thus the foundation of the Devonshire Association for the advancement of Science, Literature and Art, as it styled itself in full, was assured.[1]

'To give a stronger impulse, and a more systematic direction, to scientific enquiry in Devonshire, and to promote the intercourse of those who cultivate Science, Literature, or Art, in different parts of the county' were its declared objects. The annual subscription was a modest ten shillings; life membership, five pounds.

When the question of choosing a president for the first year had been discussed, someone had suggested Sir John Bowring. Sir John was duly invited, accepted, and gave the inaugural address at the first general meeting, held in Exeter in August, 1864. Sixty-nine members (all men — no women joined until later) attended, and six papers were read.

Sir John Bowring was a linguist and traveller eminent enough to be accorded five pages in the *Dictionary of National Biography*. Born in Exeter in 1792, he was descended from an old Devon family which had prospered in the wool trade. He learned some dozen European languages, including Russian and Magyar, and travelled widely in Europe, the Middle East and Far East , acquiring more languages as he went (he was said to have a thoroughly good knowledge of about forty by the end of his life). Most of his early journeys were connected with his own business interests, but as time went on he was sent on commercial missions by the government. During periods in Britain he was elected M.P. for Kilmarnock in 1835 and for Bolton in 1841. An early enthusiast for decimal currency, he was influential in bringing about the addition of the florin to English coinage as what he hoped would be a first step towards decimalization. When appointed British Consul at Canton in 1847 he added Chinese to his list of languages, but ten years later hostilities with China led to his barely escaping with his life. Beside all his work in public life he published some three dozen books on a variety of subjects — including, naturally enough, travel and translations of poetry and prose from several languages, as well as a quantity of verse and a number of hymns. He was co-editor and later editor of the prestigious 'Westminster Review'. He was knighted in 1845 and honoured with many foreign decorations.

His inaugural address to the Devonshire Association wandered over a number of subjects; at the end he apologised for its desultory character, regretting that his 'shattered health had not allowed him adequately to respond to the flattering invitation which had given him the opportunity of addressing them'. Four years later, his health evidently restored, he read a paper to the Association which was included in the first volume of its Transactions. It had the title 'Language, with Special Reference to the Devonian Dialects'. In this he said 'Half a century ago, the county of a country gentleman was easily discoverable wherever he went', but he thought that before long 'all provincial idioms would be absorbed into one national language' as the result of the 'constantly growing facilities of intercourse, the progress of education, the reading of books and newspapers, and generally by the spread of knowledge, and the development of thought.' For all that, if a vocabulary were constructed 'to consist of local Devonian words —meaning words not found in the English dictionary — of words which though found in them, have a peculiar local meaning — and of words whose form and pronunciation are so unlike our common English as not to be intelligible to Englishmen in general, that vocabulary would consist of nearly two thousand words.' Perhaps thinking of the 'Exmoor Courtship' and 'Scolding', he drew attention to the 'superfluity of words having the same meaning, as pulking, lamming, strapping, swinging, thumping, wopping. walloping. all meaning, when applied to a man, a stout, coarse fellow.'

Despite Sir John's interest, and although the Association began to set up committees to study such subjects as the meteorology of Devon, Scientific Memoranda and Devonshire Folklore, no move to establish one on dialect was made until in 1875, three years after Sir John's death, William Pengelly, who had been one of his close friends, read a paper on 'The Verbal Provincialisms of South-West Devonshire' at the Association 's meeting at Torrington. As a result of his influence a committee on 'The Verbal Provincialisms of Devon' was set up in 1877. He was one of its seven members, all of whom came from the south of the county except George Doe of Torrington.

Contributions were invited from Association members, and guidelines were published; the sort of words wanted were those not occurring 'in a good English dictionary of the present day', or if so occurring, used in a sense different from any definition of the word given in the dictionary. Dialect names of animals, vegetables or things were welcome, as well as phrases or expressions. Contributors were asked to say where and when each recorded 'provincialism' was heard in speech or seen in writing, to accept nothing second-hand, to give the sex, occupation and age of the speaker, and to avoid all attempts at derivation. An example of the sort of thing the committee wanted was provided: 'Fleeches (= large flakes. Rhymes with breeches.) A servant girl, native of Prawle, South Devon, residing in Torquay, and about 21 years of age, stated in March, 1877, that the snow was falling in fleeches, meaning large flakes. She added that small flakes were not fleeches.'

Members evidently responded with enthusiasm: the first report on 'verbal provincialisms' in 1877 offered 123 words and phrases, and by 1913, when an index was published, more than 3,000 words had been reported. Some of these, however, did not belong exclusively to Devon, and others were simply Devonshire mispronunciation of words in common use. From then on until the present day, most volumes of the Association's transactions have contained a number of dialect words, although it was not until 1963 that the phrase ''verbal provincialisms' was replaced by the simple word dialect.

Not all those who took an interest in dialect, of course, joined the Association. Lists of members' names were published annually. That of Sarah Hewett, author of *The Peasant Speech of Devon*, published in 1892, does not appear among them, but her book, which included a glossary of just over a thousand words, shows close knowledge of the speech of Devonians, especially in the examples she gives for the use of each word.

In the national census for 1881 for Tiverton, Sarah Hewett, from Torquay, appears as the head of a household at Wilderness House in Berrington Street, Tiverton. She was forty years old, and a widow. She ran Wilderness House as a small private boarding school; her domestic staff included a housekeeper, two housemaids and a cook. No doubt she did a good deal of the teaching herself, helped by an English governess, a German governess and a music governess. Some of her 24 pupils came from as far away as Tipperary, Pembroke and Abergavenny (one, Minnie Hall, came from Assam; perhaps her parents were tea planters).

In her preface to the first edition of her book she said she had spent a quarter of a century in collecting the words and sentences of which it was composed. '. . . having moved about amongst the people in every corner of "dear old Devon" I record that which I have heard without the desire to claim originality or exclusiveness . . . The speech of the peasantry of Devon and the adjacent counties is undoubtedly the purest remains of the Anglo-Saxon tongue extant in England at the present time.' She considered that Devonians were unrivalled for 'high buoyant spirits and dare-devil recklessness' and that 'high or low, rich or poor, all are brimful of fun and bubble over with laughter-provoking jokes'. However she, like Sir John Bowring and others, thought that 'The so-called higher education of the working classes was swiftly and surely banishing the Saxon element from our midst.'

A second edition followed soon. In the preface to this, Mrs Hewett said that 'the unexpected rapidity with which the first edition of my unpretending book was taken up has made it necessary to prepare a second for the press within some six months.' She had taken the opportunity of making a careful revision of the whole work. '. . . from all ranks of society the book has met with gratifying evidence of sympathy' and there had been many kind notices. Yet she considered that its sole claim was 'as a faithful record of the homely Devon speech, and that as such it has been accepted by Devonians all the world over, cannot but fill a Devonshire woman with pride. If it leads those who have left their native county in search of success elsewhere, to think again of the home of their childhood, and to recall its racy accents to their ears, the leisure of many years will not have been spent in vain.'

She began with a few hints on pronunciation. 'In most words "oo" takes the sound of the modified German "u" — (She distinguished such words by using the German umlaut over the 'u' — boot, büte, foot, füte, cook, cüke). When "oo" was followed by 'r', the second 'o' was changed to 'a'; door became doar, poor, poar, etc. Words such as beauty and view also took the 'ü' — büty, vü.

She noticed the tense of the verb 'to be': future, 'I be agwaine vor to be, 'er will ago vor to be, and us chell go vor to be'. For the future perfect she gives, 'I chell 'ave ben and gone vor tu du't (it is noteworthy that she shows the vestigial 'ich' sound as still in use in the 1890s) , and for the subjunctive she gives 'Ef zo be as yu be there, wullee tell 'n?; and for the imperative, 'Yu let 'er be,' 'letten 'lone' and 'layve un bide.' 'A' took a long sound — fat, fa-at, want, wa-ant'. 'H' before 'e' was sometimes pronounced as 'y' — heat, yet, heath, yeth. 'Ee' was often added to verbs — hop, hoppee, tell, tellee, sit, zittee and listen, listenee.

The past tense of verbs was formed by simply adding 'ed' — gone, goed, do, dued, came, comed. hurt, hurted.

She listed interjections: 'My Eyemers!' 'Criminy!' 'Wurrah!' and 'Aw, dallybuttons'.

Despite her fear that dialect was dying out, she observed that 'gentlemen of the old school type make it a practise to speak the native dialect when they meet at convivial reunions'.

In a section of her book headed 'Old-fashioned Rectors and their Doings' she included two anecdotes showing parsons using broad Devon. Asked why he had not married a lady instead of a farmer's daughter, one of them answered, 'Why, man-alive, duee zim I want'th to die avore mi time? . . . if I'd a married a vine-vingered lady, her mid 'ave a-zent the game tu table in a most unstomickable fashion. Now, thease du knaw stuffing vrom nattlings.' (Nattlings were pigs' intestines, now usually known as chitterlings.)

Another parson — was it perhaps the Revd John Russell? — asked 'Where are you off to this morning?' replied, 'Oh, I'm off to Whipshire (Tiverton) tu judge tha dugs. I dawnt knaw nort about lapdugs an' mastiffs, but if 'twas a vox-ound, or a tarrier dug, I cude a-dued it wi' any man in the county; but sheep dugs an' tha rest aw'm, why, I know'th jist so much about um as a cat knowth about his grandfather!'

Like Defoe, she had heard a passage from the Bible rendered in dialect, though in this case the reader was an old man, not a schoolboy; she quotes his version of Matthew VIII, 3-9: 'Be'old a zawer went vorth tu zaw; an' when 'e zawed zom seeds valled by the wayside, an' tha vowls comed an' picked um awl up; zom valled up, pintap ov stony places, where they hadden a-got much airth; an' vothwith they springed up, they wuz scarched: an cus they hadden a-got no rutes they wuthered away. An' zom valled amung therns, an' tha therns springed up, an' chucked um: But uthers valled intu gude groun' an' brat voth frute, zom a 'underedvold, zom zexty-vold, zom thertyvold. He that hath yers tu yer, lett'n yer.'

(Frederic Elworthy, in the preface to his edition of the Exmoor dialogues, said many of the clergy 'even now, when dialects and provincialisms are supposed to be dying out, men too of real culture and large knowledge, are unable to throw off their native brogue, and quite unconsciously make their 's's' into 'z's' and their 'f's' into 'v's'. One I know well always reads 'A zower went vorth to zow, etc.' Yet of course he would not write thus'.)

Sarah Hewett included a letter of invitation written to a Mr Baker, of Guzemoor Barton, Thongsleigh, Near Holsery, to his friend Bill Hodge. Like the letter written by a 'South Devon lady' reproduced in chapter four, it is not wholly convincing in its phonetic spelling — as Richard Chope put it, 'not as an imitation of a letter written by a peasant, but rather to show how such a person would talk.'

'Dear Bill

i now zits down and takes up my pen tu rite yu thease vew lines, oping it wil fine yu quit wel, as et layves me at preysent, thank God vor et.

Us've a-killd (sic) a peg, 'ers aiteen scor, an' us wants yu an' Sara tu com out next Zinday an' 'ave a bit an' a drap wi' us. Tez a fery long time agone, yu com'd auver yer, an' us du zim yu mid com an' 'ave zom diner. Ef yu 'ave got zom airly tatties that be a prim zort bring um along wi' 'e an' i can changee cuz i've a-got zom buties ov Abrim i can letee 'ave insteyd'.

This was followed by a little dialogue scene, 'The Invitation Accepted'. It begins with Mrs Baker opening the door to her friends.

"'Aw, my dear life, yu be com'd tu last! I be zo glad tu zee 'e. Us 'ad a-gived 'e up; thort yu wadden a-coming at aw! Where's Bill gone tu?"

Mrs Hodge: "Aw, 'e's a-coming; 'e's behind telling tu Mr Baker."

Mrs Baker: "Niver min' 'e; com' along upen chimmer (bedroom) and take off yer bunnit."

Mr Baker to Mr Hodge: "'Ullaw, Bill! howst a-gitting on? Come in 'ouze, duee. Yer, yer, 'ang up yer 'at, an' bring a cheer auver 'side the vire. I zim 'tes cowld nuff for snaw!"

Mr Hodge: "In tha zin 'tes turrabul 'ot, but tha wind blaw'th cowld in tha shade an' roun' tha cornders, tho' tez ferry fine vor tha time of yer. Purty gude sayzon."

Mr Baker (calling upstairs): "Now then, missis, bantee coming down to take up tha dinner? Tha crock is purty near bowled dry."

Mrs Baker: "Aw, 'ess, I be coming; duee 'ave pashins vur a minit till Mrs Hodge 'ave righted 'erzel up a bit."

Mrs Baker, having dished up the dinner, arranges 'tha mayte, pudden, greens and tatties' and pours out the cider.

Mr Baker: "Now then, sose, sit round. Yu, Bill, zit next tu my missis, and Mrs Hodge duee com' up yer aside o' me. I'll take care ov yu, and Bill, yu luke arter my missis. A chaange's gude vor boath o'us."

Mr Hodge: "'Ees, to be zure! 'Ot yu zay 'bout it, Mrs Baker?"

Mrs Baker, blushing: "Git 'long wi' yer rummage, du! Yu tu ol' fellers be like tu bwoys, thof yu be zo gray's badgers."

Mr Hodge: "Zo yu've killed yer peg, I zee. 'Ow did 'er turn out?"

Mr Baker: "Aw, us didden wey un, but shud thenk 'e wuz between vifteen an' twenty score. 'Tes licking gert 'ams."

Mr Hodge: "Howzimever, this yer is a rare bit ov pork. 'Tez rich and tasty-like."

Mrs Baker: "I tellee 'ot tes. I'll gie 'e zom ov tha nattlings tu take 'ome wi' 'e. Ya nidden be aveared they bayn't clayne, vor I wash'd um my ownzel."

Mr Hodge: 'Ow bout they tatties yu wrote about? I've a-brot a few elefants an' skulemasters tu change vur your buties ov Abrims."

Mr Baker: "Thankee, thankee! I 'opes as 'ow us chell 'ave a gude crap! I 'ad dree score to tha yard last yer. 'Ot's become ov your Charlie? I ant a-zeed 'n vur a brave while now."

Mr Hodge: "Aw! he's gone tu zey aboard a man-o-war, bound vur tha Hinges, an' Silas is a-go vur a hoss-sodger."

Mr Baker" "Aw, poor blids, I zim 'tweel be a longful time avore yu zee'th uther wan ov um again!"

The men, having finished dinner, retire to the 'chimbly cornder' to smoke and drink. The women clear the table, tidy up the room, and saunter about the garden, having a gossip until it is tea-time, when Mrs Baker, coming into the room, says in a bright cheery voice: "Now then, yu men-vokes, put up yer churchwardens an' zit vore an' 'ave som tay. Yu be like a passel ov ol' wimmen when yu git'th together. Yu tell, tell'th till awl's blue!"

Mr Hodge: Well, us dawn't meet vury offen, an' when us do us vurgits the time! Nuther thing, us bant fond ov tay. I never titches et ef I can git a drop ov gude cider, an' maister's yer be a prime zort."

As soon as tea was over and twilight set in, a move was made to put on 'bunnit an' coat'.

Mrs Hodge (to her husband): "Now then, Bill, let's shet away 'ome avore dark."

Mr Baker: "'Ot's yer hurry, missis? Yu midden niver come again."

Mrs Hodge: "Aw, niver mind that, us'll be agwaine now, plaize. Us chell be very glad to zee yu and Mrs Baker awver tu zee us zoon: yu'll be very welcome. Dare zay us'll be able to vind zummat tu aite an' drink!"

Mrs Baker: "Thankee, thankee zhure! Us'll come zum day when tes vull mune: then us chell 'ave a light coming 'ome."

All shake hands two or three times over, and seem never to be able to say 'Goodbye', till Mr Hodge starts off in boyish style, exclaiming: "Nightee gude wishee! Nightee gude wishee! I'll urn 'ome and leave the tu wimmen-vokes to tell out their tale, Now then, Polly, come on, duee!"

Sarah Hewett gives the date of this little dialogue as April, 1888.

A section headed 'Local Phraseology' forms the greater part of *The Peasant Speech of Devon*. It takes the form of some 800 dialect words and phrases, each followed by an example of its typical usage. The following is a selection.

Ammil, hoarfrost, when it settles on trees and shrubs. 'Düee lükee; zee tha trees be lüking bütival 's marning. Lükes 'z ef they wuz covered wi' dimonds. Us dawn't offen zee the ammil za thick, dü us?'

Busky-eyed, intoxicated. 'Lükee zee tü Billy Blake! I'm baggered ef 'e idden busky-eyed again, an' 'e tüked tha pledge only last week. Ther's yer taytottallers again! They taketh kindly tü liquor.'

Crams, two meanings, creases or fidgets. 'Yu've a-cramed yer vroks purty well; I can tellee they lüke's thof they'd been drawd drü a ca've's mouth', but also 'Git along, dü! Yu got za minny crams, yu dawnt knaw whot yu want'th,'

Drabbited, bad-tempered. 'Awl I can zay vur tha drabbited little twoad is that 'er shetten come yer again vur zome time tu come, I warndee!'

Fainty, oppressive weather. 'I zim tha weather's cruel fainty tü-day, zir. Ther's thinder about. I veels wangery.' (limp or weary)

Frawsy, a dainty feast. 'Now awl tha vokes be ago tü races, us'll 'ave a frawsy awl tü oursels. What chell us 'ave?

'Aw, let's 'ave a fowl an' a figgy pudden.

'Zo us will.'

Goodied, benefited. 'Vokes be zaying that Mr Moral Mackanzie (sic) is ago awver tü zee tha emperor, I'll warndee he'll goody purty much by thickee job, ef 'e ant a goodied a'ready.'

Hadge-tacker, a repairer of hedges. 'Varmer Bulley's acomed tü zometheng; they zay 'e's nort but a hadge-tacker now, an' work'th vur his dairyman that wuz.'

Item, a trick. 'Her's za vull ov items as a egg's vull ov mayte.'

Jit, might mean an upward twitch, a push or a sharp slap.'Gie 'n a little jit; he'll go vast 'nuf then' or 'I ant a-hurted tha bwoy. I only gie'd 'n a jit in tha niddick.'

Kerpee, to find fault (derived from carping?). 'I cudden live wi' Bill Cox's wive (sic) vur a year tü zave my life. 'Er dawnt du nort but kerpee, kerpee, vrom one week's end tu another. I'd zunder 'ang myzel than put up wi't.'

Lowster, to work laboriously. 'I got tha best wive in tha worr'ld. 'Er's wan that lowsters about tha 'ouze awl day long. None ov yer squatting about till tha work's a-düed.'

Maygames, frolics. 'Yu niver did zee sich a feller in yer life. 'E dawnt dü nort vrom cockcraw tü zunset, but be up tü awl zorts ov maygames. There idden a bit ov harm in en tho'.

Murchy, mischief. 'Thickee young hoseburd ov a squire is up tü a burned sight more murchy than 'is vather wuz. That' s needless tu, I'm dalled ef idden.'

Mickling, taking short steps. 'Whotiver be yü mickling along like that vur? Düee stap out, or us shan't git 'ome avore dark. I can't abide zich mimpsy-pimpsy ways.'

No-tany-by, no-tino-by, no-tano-by, no, of course not. 'I zay, Bill, yü bant agwayne tü church thease marning, be 'e?' 'No-tany-by! tidden wo'th while tü go tü listenee tü zich an old drummeldrane (bumblebee) as 'e is.'

Pilth, fluff. 'When yu'm sewping (sic) out tha chimmer, Liza, düee mind an' sewp up awl tha pilth vrom under tha beyds.'

Quelstering, sweltering. 'Aw Jiminy! idden et a quelstring 'ot day? I'm za 'ot's Mally Palmer, an' 'er cudden say 'er prayers vur tha yett.'

Ranticumscour, an uproar. 'Now then, yü rascals, whot's awl this ranticumscour about?' Other words given a similar meaning are ramgasking, rumbullioning and ragrowstering. (The latter could also be simply rowstering.) 'Whot the dowl düee mayne by awl this ragrowstering noise? Zit down thease minit, an' hold yer row.'

Skriddick, a remnant. 'Well, they've eyte awl tha mayte; there idden a skriddick alayved.' Similarly snickit meant a very small piece. 'I only wants just a snickit. 'Tez tu match me bunnet strings tu me gownd. Tha leastest morsel'll dü.'

Sküte, a reward or tip.

Sproil, strength. 'Aw dear! I be most a-düed up. I ant got wan bit ov sproil a-layved in me.'

Tankerabogus, a bogie. 'Now, Polly, yu've abin a bad, naughty maid, an' ef yü be zich a wicked cheel again, I'll zend vur tankerabogus tü come an car yü away tu 'is pittee-awl.

Thurdled, meagre. 'Aw, poor blid! 'E's a poor thurdled-stommicked theng. Luke's 'z ef 'e wuz 'alf-starved.'

Ummits, large pieces. 'Willee plaize tü gie us some tidy-zized ummits ov burd an' cheese vur vornoons tu-day.'

Umpsouze. Sarah Hewett was told by an old woman, with tears of joy in her eyes, that she'd been given a place in the umpsouze, or almshouse.

Vady, tainted. 'Us can't ayte this yer mayte, 'tez za vady.'

Watter-swate, clean. 'I ant a-scrubbed tha back-'ouze tü-day; I've just gie'd 'n a lick an' a promish till Zatterday. 'Tes watter-swayte, any'ow.'

Waxing curls, swollen glands. 'Why idden your little maid tü sküle tü-day then?'

'Aw, poor little blid, 'er idden very well, 'Er waxing curls be down, an' I've a-bin rubbing um back wi' 'arts-orn an' oil.'

Wee-wow, crosswise, puckered or squinting. 'Thease seam is awl wee-wow,' or ''Er babby's eyes is drefful wee-wow like.'

Yark, sprightly. 'Aw, my bwoy, yu be lüking yark s'marning. Whot's up wi' 'e?

Zawk, a silly person. 'I call'th 'e a proper zawk, I dü; 'e dawnt knaw great A vrom a 'oss's 'ead.'

Zogging, dozing. 'I dawnt zim 'e's azlape, 'e'th a-bin zogging this longful time.'

Many of the illustrations of the way individual words might be used are not only interesting in themselves, but often include particular examples of grammar or spelling. For instance, among those just quoted there is an example of the typical Devonian formation of the past tense of a verb (tüked for took) and the old 'th' added to the third person singular (tak'th, want'th, work'th). Not only is metathesis (the reversed 'r' sound) shown in 'burd' for bread, but a more unusual reversal, 'sewping' for sweeping, appears in relation to 'pilth'. It is somewhat surprising to find the vestigial 'ich' being included a late as the 1890s ('What chell us have?') Similarly 'thof' for though might have been expected to have died out by the end of the 19th century.

In addition to *The Peasant Speech of Devon*, Sarah Hewett wrote *'Nummits and Crummits*, first published in 1899 — by which time she seems to have given up her school, as she was living at 3 Blundell's Crescent, Tiverton, (possibly she had obtained some kind of post at Blundell's School). A London publisher brought out a new edition of this second book under the title, *Devonshire Stories. Fairies and Superstitions* in 1900. Chapter titles were: Superstitions, Things Lucky and Unlucky, Charms, Customs, Weather Lore and Wise Saws, Nummits and Crummits, Peculiar and Eccentric Devonians, Stories and Old Songs. The book's original title came from a traditional saying concerning meal times: 'A wee-bit and breakfast, A stay-bit and dinner; A nummit and a crummit, and a bit arter supper.'

One of the most striking of the many anecdotes in the book recalls Thomas Hardy's wife-selling character, Michael Trenchard, in *The Mayor of Casterbridge.* In 1810 a newspaper reported, under the heading 'The Sale of Effects and a Wife', that John Smale of Plymouth had received four pounds ten shillings from Edward Salter 'for goods received and chattels, a bay mare, and also Mrs Smale, as parting man and wife.' This was agreed before four witnesses, all of whom made their mark instead of signing their names, as did John Smale. There was a sequel: John Smale decided that he wanted his wife back. In May, 1811, Edward Salter was advised by magistrates to give up Mrs Smale, although he said that he liked her very much, and did not want to part with her. (What Mrs Smale felt about the whole matter is not mentioned.) Remarkably, as late as March, 1894, the 'Western Morning News' reported that the deserted wife of a man who had emigrated to Australia agreed that she should be offered for sale. With a halter round her neck she was led into the marketplace 'accompanied by a crowd of persons. No bidders, however, seemed to be amongst them, and the woman was obliged to be content. This disgraceful scene was witnessed by a very large number of spectators.'

Another, undated, 'Western Morning News' item concerned a man whose pet goose was stolen. He identified the bird, saying, 'If I cal'th she, her'll know my voice and answer me back.' Moreover, he said, 'I've a-had she for purty nigh ten year and I widden take ten pounds for 'er. Why, my old 'oman lovth her so well's her du inny of our children. I mayne tu take 'er 'ome wi' me and keep 'er so long's 'er liv'th, ess fy! 'Er'll sit in the chimbly cornder warm and comfortable like.'

Having proved in court that the goose, called Sallie, did indeed rush to her master as soon as he called her name, 'clearing every impediment', he was admitted to be her owner and the case against the man who had stolen her was proved.

Chapter Six

A late Victorian View: 'Devonshire Idyls'

The 1890s saw the publication of two books of stories of Devon rural life by a contemporary of Sarah Hewett, Hannah Cox O'Neill, author of *Devonshire Idyls* and *Told in the Dimpsies.* Her father, a missionary, had retired to Lynton, where Hannah, the youngest of his five children, was born in 1832. She became a teacher, but later was drawn to nursing, and served for some time as a district nurse at St Albans. Her final post was as head of a government hospital. With another nurse she wrote *Our Nurses, and the Work they do* and *New Life, its Genesis and Culture,* a book for young mothers. It seems that she did not turn to writing about the people of her native county until she retired.

In 1900 she moved to Mortonhampstead. The rector of the neighbouring parish of North Bovey was the Revd Thornton, who had been curate of Lynton when she was a girl; they had remained friends ever since. His *Reminiscences and Recollections of an Old West Country Clergyman* is dedicated to her.

She was described as tall, with bold features and a very kindly expression. She was always bright and vivacious, and when she entered a room the company seemed to feel that an exceptional personality had come into their midst. She spent her last years in Mortonhampstead, where she died in 1915.[1]

The third edition of *Devonshire Idyls* was brought out in April, 1892, by Gibbings and Company of London, but its Devon distributor was the Exeter publisher, Henry Eland, who would later publish the early works of 'Jan Stewer' (A.J. Coles). In a short preface, Hannah O'Neill observed that 'Impressionists of the new school, reading their own melancholy into a humanity they look at with contemptuous pity, would fain have us believe that life is scarcely worth living on any terms — certainly not, when money is short, and food means daily toil, and the care of children interferes with preconceived notions of love and pleasure.

In these days of hurry and competition, there is no doubt that the "art and joy of humble life", as Ruskin puts it, is in danger of being lost from among us. Half a century ago, there were traces of such an art existing in many a Devonshire home, where dwelt simple country folk lapped in sweet content.

These tales relate some of the incidents of those bygone times. They would have no merit if they were not absolutely true, except in unessential details of name and place.'

Today it would certainly be regarded as absurd, by most people of the industrial world, that there could be an 'art and joy' in humble life and poverty, or that simple country folk could ever have lived 'lapped in sweet content.' *Devonshire Idyls* might therefore be dismissed as an idealised picture of a Devon that never existed.

Yet the stories bear witness to a self-sufficient way of life in which people accepted their very limited means as inevitable, and got along as best they could. And reports prepared for the Board of Agriculture, established towards the end of the 18th century, suggest that country people in Devon were indeed reasonably content with their lot. Robert Fraser, whose *General View of the County of Devon, with Observations on the means of Improvement* came out in 1794, made the point that the division of land into small farms 'tended to increase the population and diffuse happiness'. He thought there was an 'openness of heart and mildness of character in the inhabitants of Devon' and a 'general urbanity of manners, and desire to please and meet the wishes of the stranger, prevail among all classes of the community, from the peer to the peasant.' Another report, prepared by William Marshall in 1796, remarked that the inhabitants of north Devon were 'civilised and intelligent'; farmers were 'mostly plain, decent-looking, working husbandmen'. Devonians in general were 'mostly of good person, tall, straight, and well-featured. Many of the women are of elegant figure'. He thought well of all he saw: 'Of the face of this fair county it were impossible to say too many fine things. But as its goodly features might lose much of their force in my own description, I will briefly set down what its happy inhabitants believe and assert it to be — "the richest finest county in the world"'.

Of the six stories in *Devonshire Idyls*, all told in the first person, the title of 'The School and its Scholars' is self-explanatory, and 'A Story of Something' is a tale of an ill-wishing that results in alarming poltergeist activity. The others outline the life stories of four people, two men and two women, all rather older than the narrator, and so born early in the 19th century. One of the men is a farmer, one of Marshall's husbandmen who, by working hard, has ensured that he and his family have never been in want. Similarly, one of the women, the widow of a miller and herself once a baker, has been thrifty all her life, and so now she is turned of seventy-six, she is living in comfort.'

By contrast a less fortunate widow, in her eighties, has to make do on an allowance of one shilling and sixpence a week from the parish, and whatever she can earn by knitting, selling fruit from her garden and, having always been 'flippant on her feet', going on errands for people in the neighbourhood, for which she is often paid in kind with eggs, bacon and cake. Her one advantage is that she lives in her own cottage, built by her husband before their marriage of the traditional cob, with a thatched roof. Yet Hannah O'Neill maintains that the old woman 'never wanted for anything while she was alive. "What can a body want more than a full belly, and a warm back, and a good thatched roof over their (sic) heads?" she was wont to say,' and after her death the narrator concludes that she had had a 'a long life and a hard one, but never a discontented or an abject one. With no luxuries and but few comforts, she lived out an honest life, and died as became a woman who respects herself.' Such country people made few demands on their environment, but their lack of acquisitiveness, now regarded as deplorable poverty, is unacceptable to Keynesian economists.

Another, younger woman, the wife of a farm labourer, explains to Miss O'Neill how she manages on his earnings of 'twelve shillings a week in winter, and fourteen or fifteen in hay-time and harvest', when she has half a dozen children to feed.

'You see, miss, my man he's never idle, he isn't. He's up with the daylight, and often before it, and he keepeth the garden splat always tilled; and we've a rare lot of taties this year, and green stuff, and that more than us can eat. And so us make shift to keep a pig now. Chris he had a fine slip of a pig from master, and he let un go very reasonable to we. There were nine shillings I'd earned up to Barton by charing, and that just paid for un. And what with the small taties, and the cabbages and garden stuff, what we'd plenty of as I boiled down for un, he didn't cost us a farthing till I put un in to fat a month before Christmas, and then 'twas four shillings for barley meal. And he *was* fat. He made eight score and over, he did, when us weighed un. And us lived on chitterlings and such-like for pretty nigh a month. The best part of the loin, I sold fresh in to Combe, and made near six shillings for it — most enough to buy a new slip with. But I wanted that money bad enough to go against the boys' boots. Shoe-leather's the hardest thing to come by, and us can't go barefoot. Then I made up some hog's puddings, too, and they bought 'em to parsonage, and that was another two or three shillings to go for shoemaker George. And the rest I put in pickle, and it 'll last us well on to Michaelmas, I reckon. Us never looks to have fresh meat, but a bit of pork is tasty like for dinner with the cabbage and that. Sometimes, if I'm lucky in selling a few flowers in to market, or mushrooms, or worts, or the few blackberries the childer pick in the Fall, I buy a bit of suet and make 'em dumplings for when the pig-meat's done. and so us gets along to Christmas again. And what I gets by a day's washing in and out with the farmer's wives, I puts it all by for clothing for Chris. He must go decent, he must; and after I've bought the bushel of wheat out of his wages, and got it ground to mill, and paid for a drop of barm for the hefting, and just a candle and that to shop, there's not much left. I got a stock of bees, too, last year and Chris he's ordered up a fine bee-butt for 'em; and I reckon to make nine or ten shillings of the honey this year, let alone a drop of metheglin for ourselves — it's handy at Christenings and such-like. One wishes to pass a compliment round when the gossips come home from church. And as for firing, the childer brings in a goodish bit of sticks and furze stumps; and master, he lets Chris have a load or two of turf when the horses ain't so busy and can fetch it in. For Chris, he's not one to make a fuss about working after hours when rain's coming and the hay out, and the master he maketh it up to un one way or another. And vearns and fuz for yetting the oven us can always have for the cutting. Yes, miss, it's a tight fit some whiles; but us never lets the little ones go hungry to bed, and the likes o' we don't look to live like gentry.'

This narrative brings to mind Flora Thompson's account, in the first chapter of *Lark Rise to Candleford,* of how an Oxfordshire village housewife made do on a few shillings a week at about the same period.

Haytime and harvest not only meant some increase in the farm worker's wage, but were also the time when he — and often his wife and children, glad of the chance to add a shilling or two to the family's income — ate perhaps six meals, or at least snacks, each day. Like Sarah Hewett, Hannah O'Neill quotes the traditional list of these, in a slightly altered form:

'Fore-bit and breakfast,
Rear-bit and dinner;
Nummit and crummit
And a bit after supper.'

She remarks that she heard old folks sneer at the newly-introduced mowing machines, 'taking the bread out of poor folks' mouths' but, perhaps wilfully mistaking the meaning of 'bread', will have none of it: 'Bread! It was cake as well , let alone gingerbread and pies, that were carried out into the fields for "nummit and crummit" when I was a little girl and used to visit at Buzacott Farm.' (As she says elsewhere, this was in the 1840s; she would then have been between eight and eighteen.)

She may be accused of sentimentality. The darker aspects of human behaviour do not appear in her stories: in fact the word behaviour occurs in them in the Devonshire sense of good manners and consideration for others. Her people 'learn behaviour' as children at home, and the lesson is reinforced by 'governess' at the village school. The title she chose indicated how, looking back, she wanted to portray Devon village life in the first half of the 19th century, however far from idyllic it may have been for some.

As the extracts quoted indicate, she seldom bothered to reproduce the speech of her characters phonetically, either in this book or in *Told in the Dimpsies,* which came out a year later. There are only a limited number of specifically Devonshire words in the stories, obviating the need for a glossary. The meaning of words such as 'goyle' (a small hollow), 'nympingang' (whitlow), 'boneshave' (sciatica or rheumatism), 'planches' (floorboards), 'douted' (extinguished), 'upping-stock' (mounting block) are left to be deduced from the context, as are phrases such as 'her was a peart maid' and 'flippant on her feet'. Devon pronunciations — 'Arrants' for errands, and 'yetting' for heating are used sparingly. Yet, using the grammar, rhythms and idioms known from her childhood, Hannah O'Neill gave her speakers a Devon dialect that is convincing, while remaining easily accessible to readers unfamiliar with it. There is no reason to doubt her claim that her stories are 'absolutely true' in the sense that she portrays the essential qualities of people she knew and the way they lived.

Another writer roughly contemporary with Sarah Hewett and Hannah O'Neill was Sir John Fortescue (1859-1933). Sir John, born at Castle Hill, Filleigh, was the fifth son of the third Earl Fortescue (and ninth child of a family of fourteen). Deprived of a hoped-for military career by poor eyesight, he became a scholar, and was for many years librarian of Windsor Castle. For thirty years, from 1899 to 1929, he was at work on his *History of the British Army* which, beginning with a projected two volumes, finally reached thirteen. Byproducts of this were many other studies of military matters, including a biography of Wellington. Yet it was a very different sort of book that was published two years before he began his great history. In his quiet-toned autobiography *Author and Curator,* he records that one evening in the spring of 1897 one of his nephews, aged nine, came to him and 'blushing and stammering, asked me entirely of his own volition to write him a book'. Sir John began it next day, and managed to finish it 'at odd times and places in the next three weeks'. With remarkable speed, Macmillan published it that autumn. It is prefaced with an 'Epistle Dedicatory to Mr Hugh Fortescue'. In mock 18th century style Sir John explains that 'there was no book that I could more profitably write for you than the life of one of our own red deer, which, as they be of the most beautiful creatures to the eye, so be also the most worthy of study by the mind for their subtlety, their nobility and their wisdom' — sentiments which did not prevent the writer from hunting them to exhausted death.

Sir John and his brothers prided themselves on being bilingual, speaking broad Devon with the country people, as did sons of many Devon squires in Victorian days — and the young Fortescues were brought up as sons of a typical squire, even though their father was a peer. It is not surprising therefore that Sir John enjoyed demonstrating his mastery of dialect.

In his introduction to Henry Williamson's *Tarka the Otter* he remarked that the biographers of animals were apt to 'endow their heroes and heroines with human attributes, and make them think as human beings. I am myself a sinner in this respect . . . ' The element of anthropomorphism in *The Story of a Red Deer* is certainly greater than in *Tarka.* Sir John's animals talk among themselves, and there are class distinctions: the patrician deer, salmon and pheasants speak in standard English, while rabbits, foxes, badgers and other creatures speak a modified version of the Devon of western Exmoor.

In chapter one the red deer calf who will grow into the doomed stag-hero of the book is following his mother across the moor when a rabbit comes out of a burrow and at once begins to address the hind as 'my lady' and the calf as 'little maister'. Her praise of them both is fulsome: 'And sweetly pretty he is, my lady; and butiful you'm looking too, in your summer coat, so glossy as a chestnut, sure enough. And dear heart alive, how he groweth.

Why 'twas but a few days agone that my Bucky saith to me — I don't rightly remember how many days agone, but I mind 'twas the very day when old Greyhen up to Badgeworthy came to ask if I had seen her poult — for she's lost a poult, my lady, hath the poor soul, as your ladyship knoweth. Well, my Bucky saith to me, "Bunny," saith he, "you may depend that young maister will grow to be so fine a stag as ever was seen on Exmoor." Then without pausing an instant she called out at the top of her voice to one of the little rabbits: "Flossy-a! Come back, little bittlehead, come back, or the fox will catch 'ee!"'

When the hind asks after the rabbit's family, she is told, "I reckon we'm well. There hasn't been no man this way this long time, thanks be; and there's plenty of meat, and not too much rain. And the family's well, my lady; look to mun playing all around, so gay; and my third family this spring, my lady — that I should say so! No, I reckon I can't complain; but oh, my lady, they foxes, and they weasels! They do tell me the old vixen from Cornham Brake hath five cubs; and I can't abide a vixen — never could. And they weasels — they're small, but they'm worse than foxes. Now there's my Bucky. He can't bide home, he saith, these fine days, but must go and lie out. I says to mun, "Bucky," I says, "'Tis very well for the likes of her ladyship to lie out every day, but you should bide home to bury. But no, he would go." Well then, Bucky," I says, "I reckon that you'll grow a pair of horns like his lordship, brow, bay and trey, Bucky," I says, "and turn to bay when the weasel's after 'ee." And with that he layeth back his ears and away he goeth — Flossy-a, come back, will ee, or I'll give you what vor! Now there's that Flossy, my lady, so like her father as my two ears. She won't bide close to bury, and they do tell me that the vixen to Cornham has moved this way. It won't do, my lady, it won't do."'

Another encounter is with 'a grey old person as big as the vixen, with a long sharp nose, and a deal of white about his face, a very short little tail, and four short clumsy legs. He was waddling along slowly. "Tisn't often that I spake, but spake I will. 'Tis mortal hard that he should come and take my house. 'Tis my house, I made mun, and I digged mun. 'Tisn't right, 'tisn't rasonable."

"What is it, old Grey?" asked the Hind.

The Badger looked up and stared. Then he said, very slowly, "Aw!" drawing out the word till he could collect his wits. "Well, look 'ee, 'tis like this. Two days agone — I think 'twas two days — the old Dog Fox — you know mun, he that hath so much white to his brush — well, he cometh to me, and saith he, "Brocky," saith he — that's the name he calleth me, Brocky, friendly like, though he warn't no friend o' mine that I know of — Well, he saith "Brocky, I know of so pretty a nest of Rabbits as a Badger could wish to see. I can't dig mun out, he saith, but you can. Oh! what I would give to be able to dig like you, Brocky!" he saith. "Come 'long wi' me, and I'll show 'ee." Well now, I'll tell 'ee which way we went.."

"No. never mind that," said the Hind. "We mustn't keep you, you know."

"Aw!" said the Badger, "well, we come to the bury, and wonderful sweet they rabbits did smell, sure enough." "Now," he saith, "I'll leave 'ee." And I digged the rabbits out: I forget how many there was — eight or nine I think — I ate mun all up, I know, and very sweet they was, I won't deny that. And then I went 'oom, but bless your life, when I got there I couldn't get into mun. Oh! 'twas terrible sure enough: 'twas more than my poor nose could stand. And the old Fox he looketh out and saith, "Tis wonderful kind of you, Brocky, " he saith, "To give me your house. Mrs Vicky liketh it wonderful, she doth. Ah! I wish I could dig like you, Brocky," he saith. And he's taken my house, and here I be. 'Tisn't right, 'tisn't rasonable."'

As Brocky waddles away his voice seems to blend into that of an old Exmoor villager complaining over some action by his landlord, or a neighbour.

Chapter Seven

Richard Pearse Chope and Devon names for birds, plants and fish

The various committees of the Devonshire Association published the results of their work in its annual volumes of Transactions. That on Devon dialect words and phrases — or, as they were termed for so long, verbal provincialisms — did so intermittently during the first thirty years of its existence. The first chairman of the committee was F.W. Firth, followed in 1879 by William Pengelly. Two year later Frederic Elworthy took over and continued until 1905. He seems to have taken a somewhat despondent view of his task; he observed that 'Only by continually directing attention to the subject can we hope to keep alive the interest and attention necessary to bring from their hiding places the treasures of our local speech, so that they may be recorded and preserved from the levelling devastation of the modern Board School. At the present rate, however, it will need the whole of a very long life, for our association to accumulate anything like a fair representation of the still extant provincialisms of Devon.' However, members were not contributing enough dialect words during the late 19th and early 20th centuries to ensure that a report appeared every year. Things changed in 1909 when Charles Laycock began a remarkable record of service to the dialect collection which continued until 1942. Whereas between 1877 and 1907 there had been a dozen years when no report appeared, Laycock did not miss a year.

He died in 1943; no 'provincialisms' appeared that year or in 1944. Then Hamlyn Parsons took over, and appealed to members to help by keeping their ears open, assuring them that 'The recorder will reply with alacrity to all communications, and tell you if, and when, the words have been recorded before, and be as pleased as you are if you have found a winner'. (His successors have been Gillian Moore, who at last abandoned 'provincialisms' for 'dialect', Sandra Lello, M. Estelle Dunsford, E.T. Abell and F.J.M. Laver.)

Albert Gregory, who called himself an obscure member of the Association, brought out a reprint of 1,400 or so contributions made by members up to 1909, arranged in alphabetical order. He prefaced it with Sir John Bowring's 'Language, with special reference to Devonian Dialects', and added the lists William Pengelly had reproduced in his paper 'The Verbal Provincialisms of South-West Devon' in 1875: a total of 323 words. About 200 of these had formed an appendix to *Kingsbridge and its Surroundings* by Miss S.P. Fox, published in 1874; the remainder were from William Marshall's glossary, chiefly of agricultural terms, included in his *Rural Economy of the West of England*. The previous year's Transactions had provided an index to the first twenty-one reports on 'verbal provincialisms', comprising some 2,700 words. In 1913 Charles Laycock referred to the glossary provided by Richard Chope to 'A Devon Dialect Letter (see Chapter Four), and said that the committee had decided to include the words from this in their next index. This came out in 1925, and all the words from Chope's glossary duly appeared in it.

Richard Chope was born at his father's farmhouse, Farford, near Hartland, in September, 1862. His ancestors had been merchants who settled in Bideford in the 16th century. One of the family bought Farford in 1721. He was educated at what was originally established in 1858 as the Devon County School with the idea of providing the sons of farmers with a public school type education at a modest cost (motto: Read and Reap). After two changes of name it became — and remains — West Buckland School. Remarkably, Chope became head boy at the age of fifteen, which suggests that in those days few boys stayed on after that age. He came first out of 2,885 candidates in the Cambridge Local Junior Examination in 1877. According to his obituary in the Devonshire Association's Transactions for 1938, in 1881 he went to Trinity College with a major scholarship, 'was bracketted 20th Wrangler in 1884, and took his degree in the same year. He entered the Civil Service by competitive examination, was appointed as Assistant Examiner in the Patent Office, and in 1903 rose to be Deputy Examiner and Principal of Abridgements'.

He never lost his love for his native county. Not long before he retired in 1922 he told the annual meeting of the London Devonian Association, which he had helped to found in 1910, 'My heart is in Devonshire. I am a true Devonian. I have been in London 38 years, but I never liked London life.'

Thankfully he returned to Hartland. He bought Fosfelle, a farm near his birthplace which had belonged to John Lane the publisher, founder of the Bodley Head. (Lane was a fellow Devonian, born at West Putford, one of the little villages in the valley of the River Torridge, only a few miles from Hartland.) Fosfelle was Chope's home for the rest of his life. He never married.

In 1902 he contributed the first of many papers he was to write for the Transactions, *'The Early History of the Manor of Hartland'* and became a member of the Council. From then on he was very active in the life of the Association, becoming a vice-president (and, for the year 1926, president), serving for a number of years as one of two honorary secretaries, and editing the Transactions from 1928 to 1930. He was a member of a number of committees, notably those on Devon dialect and Devon folklore, preparing the annual reports on the latter subject from 1925 to 1936.

He wrote several books. The first, *The Story of Hartland,* he published himself in 1902, having printed it on a wooden press he had made. This edition, and a reprint, became collectors' items. He also published another short book, *Farthest from Railways,* about Hartland, then exceptional in being at a considerable distance from the rail network. He edited *Early Tours of*

Devon and Cornwall, which included extracts from the writings of many travellers, from John Leland to 'Don Espriella' (Robert Southey).

Among his papers for the Association's Transactions was 'The Book Dialect of North Devon', in which he discussed the 'Exmoor Scolding' and 'Courtship', Mary Palmer's 'Devonshire Dialogues' and William Rock's 'Jim and Nell' — observing, incidentally, that in none of these works was a regular or consistent system of phonetic spelling employed. According to his obituary, 'On the speech of his native county he was admittedly the foremost living authority'. One especially interesting contribution to dialect records which he undertook was to collect the many dialect names of birds, plants, animals and fish.'

In 1882 the Revd Hilderic Friend had published 'A Glossary of Devonshire Plant Names' in Volume 14 of the Devonshire Association's Transactions. Fifty years later, Richard Chope produced a greatly expanded glossary. He gave the English name of each plant, followed by a list of its dialect names, and finally its Latin name.

Some had as many as two dozen or more dialect names, though not all were exclusive to Devon: to take only three, among those he gave were Lent lilies for daffodils, which occurs in Cornwall and elsewhere, old man's beard for wild clematis, which is in widespread use, and weatherglass for scarlet pimpernel, the little flower known as some kind of weatherglass in other parts of England.

The most familiar flowers, naturally enough, had the most names. Herb Robert, for instance, had no fewer than thirty, including dolly's apron, pinafore, nightcap and shoes; sparrow birds, wren's flower, red bird's eye, candlesticks, and many variations of Robert and Robin. In earlier times the early purple orchis was evidently common enough to have attracted quite a few names: jolly soldiers, soldier's cap, Adam-and-Eve , goosey-gander, adder's flower and adder's tongue, cuckoo plant and the delightful gramfer-griggles. (Britten and Holland's *Dictionary of English Plant Names* says that 'griggles' appears as 'greagles' in Dorset, and comes from an old Saxon word meaning greyish-blue). Bluebells too were known as gramfer-griggles, among other things; it was not unusual for the same name to be applied to several plants. Both the early purple orchis and the cuckoo pint might be called poison-maur (root poison); bird's foot trefoil could be hen and chickens, (another of the names of Herb Robert), great bindweed, larkspur and woody nightshade might all be granny's nightcap — yet again a name for Herb Robert.

The delicate white flower of spring hedges, greater stitchwort, was sometimes known, appropriately, as Whitsun Sunday; it could also be pixy flower, star of the wood, smooth frock, billy buttons, one o'clock, lady's watches and breakhearts.

The big umbellifer usually called cow parsley — so persistent that even if it is cut down annually will continue to sprout from a root that grows year by year to the size of a parsnip — had more than twenty names. There were various spellings of kex, kexy, caxeys and so on. but it was also known as pig's bubble and pig's flop, sweet-biller, umlick and both rabbit's meat and snake's meat. Chope recalled that country people had once kept bundles of the dried stalks, called limpernscrimps or limperscrips, beside their hearths for use as spills or tapers. They are of course hollow, and boys used them as pea shooters, water squirts or drinking straws, calling them wippul-squips.

Daffodils were not only Lent lilies but Lent pitchers and Lenticups, as well as cuckoo roses, gooseflops, gracy or grassy daisies, bellroses, Gregorys and even cowslips.

Puffballs, aptly enough, could be devil's snuffboxes, pixy puffs or fuzzballs; thistles were dashels of some sort — milky dashel, horse dashel; the little plant so often seen growing on walls, pennywort, could also be penny-cakes, -caps, -leaves or -plates as well as nipplewort, dumplewort and devil's candlesticks. The grass so unwelcome to both farmer and gardener, couch grass, might be known as sproil, squitch or twitch and dog grass. Seaweeds in general were imaginatively named furbelows, and the edible seaweed still so popular in Devon, laver, was brown butter.

Chope included a few fruiting trees. There was the old cider apple, cockergee or cackergee, the quarrender or quarrington and the remarkably named cobble-dick-longer-skin. Varieties of prunus, from blackthorn to wild plum, might be known by the names of their fruits; castings, gawks, slones, gristlings., bullins and grigs. The berries of the hawthorn could be aggles, haigles, peggles and chuck-cheese. An old country rhyme ran:

'Many nits (nuts), many pits (graves),

Many sloans (sloes), many groans,

Many aggles, many cradles.'

As with flowers, the more familiar birds had the most names. The robin had about twenty, among them poor Rab, bob-berrick, boberdie and boberdick, robin-urdick, reddock or ruddock, poor man's friend, posty-legs, God Almighty's cock and farewell summer — the last presumably a reference to the robin's lovely autumn song. The wren had some three dozen names, companioning the robin as God Almighty's hen, and being known as ox-eye (as were the great tit and chiffchaff) and ackymal, like the blue tit. It might also be cock-tiddley, crackety or crackedy, cuddley, cuddy bear, cuddly-bum, kitty lodger and kilty lodger, tidley tope and, remarkably, ring-tailed roarer.

For the blue tit there were some two dozen variations on ackymal, but also blue bonnet, blue bottle, blue speck, Billy-biter, heckanoddy, tidley and even underground tiddley oxy. By some confusion with the bull-finch, it could be known as bloom- or blooth-picker.

The chaffinch's song attracted such names as chink, pink-twink and spinker, but it had many other names: apple bird, scurry, copperfinch and mazed finch.

The song thrush had fewer names than might be expected: an obvious one was specklebreast. and it was known by altered pronunciations such as drish and dirsh and drishel. Chope says it could be called the stormcock, but this of course is usually applied to the mistlethrush; similarly the mistlethrush was sometimes mistaken for the fieldfare. Both were sometimes referred to simply as grey birds. Apart from holmscreech, the mistlethrush had a number of dissimilar names: dwindo, windle, winnow and bulvare.

Pied wagtails may have been far more often seen in the countryside than they are today: they could be known as trotty wagtails, peggy or polly washdish, bottle washer, nolly or babbling titter. Yellowhammers, too, must have been numerous enough to acquire a variety of names: furze (vuz) jet, gladdy, golden-breasted chat, golden hammer, little-bread-and-no cheese (derived from its song), winky, yellow linnet and yellow yowley, among others. The beautiful little long-tailed tit had to be content with bum-barrel or bum-towel.

Among the larger birds the magpie might appropriately be called chatterbox, chatterpie or chitterpie; otherwise it could be maggie, maggoty pie, mock-a-pie, parson and, with reference to its spring-time habit, egg-stealer. The green woodpecker, for some reason, might be the wet bird, rain-bird or rainfowl; it was also galleypot, hoodwall, kickol, tick-tack, yaffle and yuckle. The kestrel was variously known as the brown hawk, crasset, mouse- or wind-hawk, wind falcon or fanner, furze kite (vuz kite) and standgate.

Only a limited number of insects seem to have been recognised: earthworms (angle-dog, angletwitch or simply angle); caterpillars (maskells); wasps (apple-dranes or apple-drones); ladybirds (cubabies); cockchafers (bumbledores, oakems or humbugs); beetles (blackworm, Devil's coach-horse, shambugs and snarly-gogs); woodlice (gramfers-grigs, recalling the gramfer-griggles accorded to bluebells and wild orchis).

As for mammals, hedgehogs were usually furze pigs (vuzpegs), squirrels were vairs (as were weasels), fairies or squiggles, badgers were boars or greys, and dormice were derrymice, churdle-crubs or shuttle-crofts and — like bats, tortoises and in some places bees — seven sleepers. Other names for bats were airymice, dairy mice, shear-a-muse, flitter mice and leatherbirds. Chope gives pollywiggle for both frogspawn and frogs, but this surely was more usually applied to tadpoles. The word 'moke' for donkey in common enough outside Devon, but malley or mulley, assneger and yessaker may be more localised.

Under 'Fish Names', Chope included crustaceans, cetaceans and molluscs. Not surprisingly, fewer marine creatures were familiar enough to have attracted many dialect names. Crabs could be umphs, velvet fiddlers, soldiers (sodgers, sojers), crabelorgins and counterfeits; the spider crab was a lacemaker. Minnows were minjies or minnies, but also silversides. Mussels were simply glams, and periwinkles, gobbets. Cuttlefish could be pollysquiggles or codells. The smallest sea bream were chad, the intermediate size ballards, and the largest, old wives. Eels, like earthworms, were angletwitches. Herrings — though only along the north coast of Devon, presumably — were Clovelly ducks. Jellyfish were blowers, bulls or bellies. The name whirlpool for a whale was evidently derived from the swirling of the sea when the great creature surfaced.

Chope's 'Dialect of Hartland' was included in volume 23 of the Devonshire Association's Transactions, having been read on his behalf by Frederic Elworthy — appropriately enough, for it is largely concerned with the fact that many words then still in use in Hartland had been marked as obsolete in Elworthy's edition of the 'Exmoor Scolding'. Chope devoted much attention to the pronunciation of vowel sounds in the Devon dialect — long and short o, long, short and open a, long and short e. He also made the point that 'the inflexion th or eth is almost invariably used with the third person singular, and occasionally with the first and third persons plural." There a go'th'; A rin'th well, dith'n a?; us caalth min Lent-rosen, but the proper name's Lent-lilies. They tell'th up all zoarts o' trade 'bout 'n."

Through his association with the English Dialect Society, Chope's name became known to students of philology outside Britain. A Methodist minister, W. Gregory Harris, wrote a number of Devon and Cornish sketches in prose and verse in the early years of the 20th century. When a selection of them was published under the title *West Country Volk,* he included an essay in which he said that a student at the University of Berlin, Bruno Scholzer, had published a book on the 'Exmoor Courtship and Scolding' and another student from the same university had studied 'Jim and Nell'; both had acknowledged indebtedness to Richard Chope.

Chapter Eight

Early 20th Century: dialect reciters and singers

Victorians and Edwardians enjoyed listening to recitations. Various kinds of entertainments, public and private concerts and what were known as Penny Readings, might include a recitation or two. Poetry was much appreciated, but so were monologues and indeed reading aloud. The material was sometimes the work of the performer (the greatest exponent of this was of course Charles Dickens, who exhausted himself on tours of performance of dramatic scenes from his own novels). In Devon, and no doubt in other counties, readings or recitations in dialect became increasingly popular. Dialect might even be used to convey information of a helpful sort. In 1885 the Society for the Promotion of Christian Knowledge published *Ways and Means in a Devonshire Village* by E. Cruwys Sharland. It consisted of tips for housewives in the form of advice given — in dialect — by Betsy Crichett, described as the widow of a coachman who had worked for many years at the 'Great House'. She was said to be regarded by her neighbours as an unfailing authority on all questions of household economy and the management of children. She also provided recipes. The SPCK brought out the book for use at Mothers' Meetings. The organisation of these usually devolved on vicar's wives; E. Cruwys Sharland may have been one of them. If she was a Devonian, she was probably well able to cope with reading aloud Betsy Critchett's useful hints, but a parson's wife from another part of the country may have deputed the job to some confident matron in the group she conducted.

The SPCK presumably made no charge for readings from *Ways and Means*, but much of the material used by dialect reciters in public performances was not only original but had already appeared in print; permission for others to make use of it could be jealously guarded.

W.S. Pasmore, author of *Tales of Devon and Cornwall,* which reached its third edition in 1900, warned readers that application for permission to recite any of the stories had to be obtained from W.H. Dalgleish, 89 South Street, Exeter, and 'all infringements would be promptly proceeded against'. Of his twenty stories, the majority are Cornish. There is also some verse, and Pasmore reproduced the words of a song for which he could not claim copyright: it was, he said, 'rendered with great éclat by the late Beadle to the Worshipful Company of Tuckers, Weavers, Fullers and Shearmen in their ancient Hall, Fore Street, Exeter, at their annual dinner on 5th November.' The Beadle had provided him with a copy of the song, called simply 'Waterloo', in his own spelling.

The first three verses ran:

' 'Twas on the eighteenth day o' June Napoleon did advance
Weth all tha choices' troops that 'e cude rise all een tha bound of Vrance.

His glitterin' 'eroes shoine around, and darin' like tha foe,
But British ly-ons stood ther' groun' on the playnes ov Waterloo.
Alow, aloo, aloo, tha' playne ov Waterloo.
Tha British ly-ons ondaunted stood ther' groun'
On tha playne ov Waterloo.

At tain o'clock tha vight commence ontil the dawn ov day
Wher' blid ov limbs and cannon bales in girt confooshun lay.
The queerceers (sic) most naubly charged awver our square to overthrow,
But British ly-ons stood ther' groun' on tha plaync ov Waterloo.
Refrain: Alow, Aloo, etc.

'Ark, 'ark, tha cheerin' off tha charge wes 'eard above tha vight
The Billyum (Belgian) trupes weth 'earts zo bad like cowards tuke tha vlight,
An' left pore Britons all alone singly with tha foe,
But British ly-ons stood ther' groun' on tha playne ov Waterloo.
Refrain: Alow, Aloo,, etc.

Although in verse four 'dreary night' came on, Wellington and 'Bloucher' nobly faced the foe, and 'Bonyparte's' emperor's crown was lost at Waterloo.' The final verse wishes peace to the 'loy'l zawls that vought that glor'yus day' and hopes that the battlefield's 'sacred clay' shall remain undisturbed so that 'tremblin' Vrainchmen' marching that way shall remember Waterloo'.

Many songs in dialect became popular. 'Widecombe Fair', in particular, must have been sung countless times. It is included in *Songs and Ballads of the West,* subtitled 'A collection made from the Mouths of the People' by the Revd Sabine Baring-Gould, which was published by Methuen in 1892. Baring-Gould said that when he appealed for contributions in local papers the only response was a score of versions of 'Widdecombe (sic) Fair'. Calling it the best known and most popular of Devonshire songs, he observed that the original Uncle Tom Cobleigh lived in a house near Yeoford Junction, and the names in the chorus all belonged to Sticklepath.

He recalled that as a boy he often rode on and around Dartmoor, and 'put up at little village taverns where he was sure to hear one or two men sing, and sing on hour after hour, one song following another with little intermission.' This would have been in the 1850s. By the time he decided to attempt his collection many of the old singers were dead, and those he could trace were near the end of their lives. However, from labourers, tin miners, moormen, thatchers and blacksmiths in Devon and Cornwall he accumulated a great number of songs, of which *Songs of the West* (harmonised and arranged by the Revd Fleetwood Sheppard) represented only a fraction of the total gathered by Baring-Gould. In 1982 the curator at the National Trust's Killerton House discovered a forgotten trove of the writer's material, as a result of which it is now known that his collection numbered some 650 songs. The Songs of West Heritage has been working to put the entire collection on microfiche in order that it may be available to public libraries.

Two songs which do not appear in the Methuen edition of Songs of the West are 'Woman's the Joy and the Pride of the Land' and 'Peggy'. The words of these are reproduced in the second edition of *Bits o' Broad Devon,* by William Weeks, who said he had taken it down from the lips of a famous old singer of Dolton, Shadrack Friend, 'a delightful baritone with a very extensive repertoire of old-fashioned songs.'

William Weeks was born at Dolton in 1855. For many years he was senior lecturer in English and maths at St Luke's College, Exeter, where he had been a student. He was usually known as Major Weeks, a rank deriving, it seems, from service in the old 1st Rifle Volunteers.

In addition to *Bits o' Broad Devon* he published *Devonshire Yarns* and *'Twas Ordained.* All three contain pieces in both prose and verse, most of which appeared in local newspapers such as the 'Devon and Exeter Gazette' and the 'Western Weekly News'; all three went into several editions. In his preface to the second edition of *Devonshire Yarns* in 1907 Weeks said that he claimed nothing for the sketches 'beyond the fact that they are careful attempts to represent with fidelity the dialect spoken in a rural district of North Devon forty years ago . . . the spelling is merely the medium by which the author endeavours to convey, as accurately as he can, the pronunciation and style of the old-fashioned North Devon villager . . . Hence there is no departure from the ordinary spelling of a word merely to make the composition look strange or "funny"; when the spelling is altered it is done solely with the object of getting nearer, if possible, to the true old pronunciation.

Some dialect writers spell "men" mane, "stone" stoan, "poor" pore, "curtain" kurtain, etc. Such changes as these seem quite superfluous, for it is doubtful whether they bring us any nearer the true sound; moreover, they have often the unfortunate effect of frightening would-be readers away by making the composition look unnecessarily strange and difficult.' Devonshire Yarns contains nineteen pieces, six of them in verse. Three of the latter had been set to music, and would doubtless have been sung at concerts by Major Weeks — who, according to his obituary, had few, if any, equals as reciter and singer of Devonshire dialect stories and songs.

Later editions of his books, like many at that time (the late 19th and early 20th centuries) carried advertisements. Among them were announcements of his other titles and also one for himself: 'W. Weeks, *Officiere d'Academie,* late Senior Tutor, St Luke's College. Author of *Exercises in Euclid* and

Characters in Shakespeare. Receives private pupils at 4 Mont le Grand, Exeter. Excellent references. Moderate terms. Lectures or Readings given for Literary Societies, etc.'

In the third edition of *Bits o' Broad Devon* (the second had been published in 1902, only a year after the first had received 'an exceedingly hearty welcome') he thanks 'all those readers and reciters who are helping to make the book more widely known. He charges no fees, though the pieces are copyright, but trusts that when one of them is given at a public entertainment the source of the contribution will either be stated in the programme or announced from the platform,.'

The Revd Gregory Harris has already been mentioned as a writer in dialect. He was the superintendent of the Wesleyan Mission in Brixham in the 1920s, but seems to have begun to write what he called his 'early impressions of country words and ways' many years earlier. His first book, *Sketches of the West Countree'* (sic) had been followed by *Down-along-o'-We* and *Zummerzet Volk and Devonshire Diversions.* All three were out of print, but in 1923 the publisher John Lane brought out *West Country Volk,* a collection of what the Revd Harris considered the most characteristic pieces. In what he calls a 'Voreword' he records that several of them had 'stood the test of public recital to interested, and therefore somewhat indulgent audiences in various parts of the country'. It seems probable that, like Weeks, he did not charge fees.

However, an Exeter bookseller and publisher, Henry Eland, most certainly did — in fact. like Pasmore, he warned that anyone intending to recite stories in collections he published must ask permission, and any infringements would be promptly proceeded against.

Henry S. Eland (the S stood for Septimus) appears in a directory of 1870 as a bookseller at 24 High Street, Exeter, but eight years later was at 237 High Street and 100 Sidwell Street, Exeter, as a stationer and owner of a circulating library and fine art gallery, as well as a bookseller. By 1914 the Eland Brothers (Henry's sons, presumably) were publishers, print sellers, news agents, booksellers and stationers, carvers, gilders, picture frame makers, picture cleaners and restorers. They claimed to have been established in 1790.

Eland published an edition of Hannah O'Neill's *Devonshire Idyls* and Nathan Hogg's *Letters and Poems in the Devonshire Dialect.* He also brought out an early collection of stories by the Devon dialect writer whose work remains unrivalled for its inventiveness and humour, *Zum Vunny Demshur Tellins* by 'Uncle Tom Cobleigh'. Later came In a *Devonshire Carrier's Van* by Jan Stewer and *Jan Stewer's Demshur Buke,* and from then on, Jan Stewer was the chosen pseudonym of the remarkable Devon dialect writer and reciter, A.J. Coles.

Chapter Nine

Early to mid-20th Century: the work of Jan Stewer (A J Coles)

Alfred John Coles, who was to use the pen name Jan Stewer throughout his writing life, was born on 14th March, 1876, at Woolwich Arsenal, where his father, a Royal Artilleryman, happened to be stationed. Nevertheless both his parents were Devonians, and he spent the greater part of his life in Devon. He left school at fourteen, worked for a time as a messenger boy, and then followed his father into the army. Strangely, in view of the long and healthy life that lay ahead of him, he was invalided out after a year or two with some supposed heart weakness. He became a school teacher, and was in charge of the little village school at Puddington, not far from Tiverton, when his first story in dialect was accepted by the editor of the 'Devon and Exeter Gazette'. It appeared just before his 24th birthday, on 9th March, 1900, under the title 'The Talk at Uncle Tom Cobleigh's Club'. It was signed Jan Stewer, and Coles received seven shillings and sixpence for it.

Some time later the editor asked for another story. Coles submitted several at irregular intervals until at last he was commissioned to produce a weekly account of discussions at his imaginary Uncle Tom Cobleigh Club, for which he was to receive ten shillings — a most welcome addition to the income of a village school teacher in 1900. At about the same time he was given an increase in salary. On the strength of this he married a first cousin, Florence Stephens, in January, 1901. According to Coles' biographer, Douglas Cook, she was a very pretty woman five years his senior. They had two sons and two daughters. By the time the elder boy was born, in 1903, Coles and his wife had moved from Puddington. During the next few years he held posts at Teignmouth, Poltimore and Bovey Tracy. In 1909 he left teaching and for four years was editor of two local newspapers, the *'Mid Devon Advertiser'* and the *'Torbay News'*. He continued to write a weekly story, although from 1905 'Jan Stewer' had been over taken over by the *'Illustrated Western Weekly News'*, for which he was to write for the next 35 years.

However, two selections from his *'Devon and Exeter Gazette'* stories were published in book form. Neither is dated, so it is impossible to know which came first, but it was probably *Jan Stewer's Demshur Buke.* The title page bears a notice saying that it has been 'Revised and Adapted for private or public reading and reciting. Reprinted from the *"Devon and Exeter Daily Gazette"*. All Rights Reserved. Printed and published by Besley and Dalgleish Ltd., 89 and 90 South Street, Exeter. Application for permission to recite any of the following Stories must be made in writing to William H. Dalgleish, South Street, and all infringements will be promptly proceeded against. Persons giving information of any such infringement to the above named will be suitably rewarded.'

There is 'Prevaace' (sic) in which Jan Stewer, signing himself 'Yours respectably' and giving his address as Uncle Tom Cobleigh's Club, Muddlecombe-in-the-Moor, confides that Uncle Tom has suggested that he should 'taake an' rite a buke', and so after initial doubts he has 'picked out aul they wat I thort yu wid like ta rade agean, an' eef yu likes thase yer, I'll mid-be led 'e 'ave zum more later on; us'll zee.' Some of the eighteen prose stories and three narratives in verse are very short, no more than three hundred and fifty to five hundred words; others run to a thousand or more. Among the prose pieces are 'Jan's Adventures with the Hot Water Bottle', ''Arry 'Awks Prize Tetties', 'Curing the Lumbago; 'Ow us med out the Census' and 'Jan's Cricket Match', which were to be included in considerably revised form in later books.

The second collection appeared as *Zum Vunny Demshur Tellins* by Uncle Tom Cobleigh. Henry Eland, like Dalgleish, inserted a warning about the need to ask permission before reciting any of the stories in public. Like his other publications, it was well supported by advertisers — more than a dozen of them, from a jeweller to a hairdresser, and including St Anne's Brewery which produced 'Uncle Tom Cobleigh brands of special Scotch whisky and Devonshire Sloe Gin.' Coles' fictional village appears in the titles of two of the twelve stories: 'Muddlecombe Rummage Zale' and 'Kursmiss Konzart tew Muddlecombe', but as in *Jan Stewer's Demshur Buke,* characters who would become so well known to Coles' readers in later years had not yet made their appearance. There is a phonetic rendering of a very broad Devon in these early stories. For instance, in 'Buller Day in Exeter', an account of the welcome given to General Buller on his return from South Africa in November, 1900, Jan is amazed at the enthusiasm of the crowd: 'Wan chap jiss 'vore me, 'e got that exzited, ev'ry time 'e drawed 'ees 'at up pin een, 'e hat me pin tha leg moas' turrable. I wid a tole un o't vor tu pins, but I wadden zartin 'ow 'e wid taake et, an' thur wadden rume tu muvvee. Wance yu was stude to a place, thur wiz no getting away vrom et.'

Coles was quickly in demand as a reciter of his own stories. According to Douglas Cock, 'His first tentative stage appearance was on 25 January 1902, in a concert at the Victoria Hall, Queen Street, Exeter (later destroyed by fire)'. It was in aid of the Journalists' Widows and Orphans Fund, and Jan's contribution was the cricket match monologue (a story that was to remain a great favourite with audiences). Soon Coles was appearing in towns and villages all over Devon, Cornwall and Somerset, giving not just a single monologue but a complete concert, 'introducing it with a description of Muddlecombe and its notable features' and making several appearances which included 'solos on a one-string fiddle made from a cigar box, a ventriloquist's sketch with Old Peter (his dummy) and a memory act.' Apparently he had not then begun to add songs to his programme, but he certainly did so later. In 1931 an edition of a collection of his stories, *Yap,* carried an advertisement at the back for 'Devon country songs, written, composed and sung by Jan Stewer.' These were 'Out come Mother and Me', described as 'a song of quaint and distinctive humour', a sequel, 'When Mother and me joined in' and 'What about a little Drop of Cider?' said to be 'very useful for an audience willing to join in a chorus'.

As has been said, in 1905 Coles moved from the 'Devon and Exeter Gazette' to the *'Illustrated Western Weekly News'*. It may be assumed that they made him a better offer than the 'Gazette's' ten shillings a story. He left the Uncle Tom Cobleigh Club behind and began a completely new series of Muddlecombe stories. Like so many villages at the time, Puddington had a carrier's cart that offered a regular service for passengers and goods to the nearest town, and Coles sometimes travelled in it. From the time Jan Stewer became a passenger in the Muddlecombe van, the wonderful cast of characters that would populate his unique world for so many years came into being — Mrs Snell, Mrs Endycott, Ned Annaferd, Lias Buzzacott and others.

There was also the carrier himself. 'Ezekiel Zalter 's name is, and so 'e orwiz goes by the naame o' Tom. I can't tell ee vor why, but 'e do wi ev'rybody, from the Squire an' passen down to the smarlees' scrallin' cheel that's able to zay anything 'tal . . . 'E draves the van an' two 'osses up to Exeter ev'ry Vriday. Starts yer-from fus' thing in the morning, an' back agaen 'bout o' zeb'n or eight o'clock o' night.' Tom carries not only eight or ten passengers but a remarkable quantity of goods: ' . . . he loads up zome pin tap the van, an' zome behind, an' zome in under. And 'e puts boxes and hampers 'pon he's own zate, an' then perches isself up pin top o' they ontil 'tis a marvel to me that he don't vall off into the rawd. And inside the van 'e heaps up the baskets, an' passels to the back, an' in under the zates . . . Tom have been loading up thick van for 'andy thirty year, and 'e knaws zackly to a ninch where the putt the things and the volks . . . I goes reg'lar in Tom's van, ev'ry wik. In fac' 'tis mostly the zame volks rides wik arter wik, cuz it comes in part of our bizness like'. Jan admits that when there happen to be two or three extra passengers, ' 'tiz a bit o' a tightish fit. But us be all jovial like, and in gude friendship.'

Tom's horses are called Damzel and Prince. ('Way-ya! Jim, jump down an' putt on the drug — right — Damzel-ah! Kimm-up 'oss. Prince-ah! Kim-eer-way. Yu maaze toad — wat' matter with ee?)'

That there might occasionally be mishaps due to the crowding in of passengers and parcels is indicated by the ending of 'The Man who never told a Lie' in the first volume of the series of three published by the 'Western Illustrated News' itself under the title *In a Devonshire Carrier's Van*. 'Well, yer us be, all change vir Muddlecombe. Come on, Missis Porter. I doan winder yu carn get up very aisy. I be darned if yu any upsaut Missis Cann's pot of traicle, an' now yule be abble to hire yerself out so much an hour as a walking fly paper.'

The 'Carrier's Van' volumes are undated, but were all published between 1905 and the beginning of the First World War. They cost a shilling, and proclaimed that Jan Stewer was writing exclusively for the 'Western Weekly News'. The three volumes contain forty-two stories in all, some of them serialised in three or four parts. Several reworked material that had appeared in *Zum Vunny Demshur Tellins* or *Jan Stewer's Demshur Buke,* such as 'The Jibbing Motor', 'Christmas Customs' and 'The Jumble Sale'.

As soon as war broke out, Coles tried to join up, despite the fact that he was thirty-eight years old. At first he was unsuccessful, but as British casualties mounted, the War Office decreed that men with previous service in the Royal Artillery might be allowed to enlist, even if over the age limit. Coles seized this opportunity. This time his medical made no mention of any heart condition. He took the precaution of memorising the sight chart, having been left alone in a room where one was displayed, in case his eyesight let him down.

Beginning in the ranks, he was later commissioned, and served in the Middle East. For a time he was in charge of a pay office in a large military camp near Alexandria. Demobilised in the autumn of 1919, he returned to the house in Torquay in which his family had been living since 1913.

He had presumably received whatever modest gratuity was appropriate to his rank at the time, and it is possible that he had a small disability pension: although he had remained a non-combatant — to his disgust, no doubt — he had been seriously ill on at least three occasions during his army service. However, for the rest of his life it seems that the greater part of his income came from his work as a writer and entertainer.

Throughout the war he had kept up the production of Jan Stewer stories, sending them back to Exeter while he was in Egypt. Sadly at least one ship carrying some of them was sunk, but Coles may have prudently kept copies. A selection appeared in book form in 1922 as *Jan Stewer at Home and Abroad.*

In his forties and fifties Coles was immensely busy. He continued his pre-war stage appearances, and as his sons and daughters grew older was able to rope them in as accompanists for his songs and as players in dramatised versions of his sketches. He gave performances in dozens of towns and villages all over the western counties, and even further afield, at Bristol, Bath, Swansea and the Midlands. (One may wonder what a Birmingham audience, for instance, made of Jan Stewer's dialect.)

Journeys by rail were often inconvenient and tiring, especially in winter, when they might involve changing trains and enduring long waits on cold stations. In Jan Stewer's words, 'Tis mortle terrifying when you get to bide fer howers to zome li'l ole station for the train to come along. Darned if I ban't beginning to know all they ole junction places off by 'art where you has to get out from one train and poke about till the nex' one arrives . . . Some of aw'm be terrible exposed, and if you got to wait fer a nower or so, the weend cuts 'ee right in two.'

Reluctantly he gave in to the opinion of friends and family that he should buy a car and learn to drive. His early experiences and mishaps with a somewhat antiquated car provided material for a series of stories, twelve of which were reproduced in *Ole Biskit*, published by Besley and Copp in Exeter in 1925. Two years later Coles acquired a London publisher for the first time, when Herbert Jenkins accepted a collection of largely rewritten early stories, and brought it out as *In Chimley Corner.* They followed this with *A Parcel o' Old Crams* in 1930, *Yap* the next year, and a new edition of *Ole Biskit* in 1933.

These four books may be seen as the quintessence of Coles' achievement as a writer. They contain many stories that provided material for his public performances ('telling up a few ole ditties to zome kickshaw or 'nother' , as he put it in the first chapter of *Ole Biskit.*) The characters established in the 'Carrier's Van' series remain much as they were before 1914, although gradually the technological changes of the 20th century impinge on their lives — wireless sets, electric light, pocket cameras, a bus in place of the carrier's van, and even the possibility of trips to that astonishing place, London, where hotels seemed like palaces, the Underground is alarming ('A feller need to be half a rabbut only to vind his way in they ole stations') and to reach it one had to go down the 'resolving staircase'. It was even possible to be terrified by going up in an aeroplane ('When Jan went Flying').

For all that Mrs Snell, who in pre-war days was astonished to see some of the Squire's female visitors wearing hobble skirts ('The 'Orrible Skirt') has still not learned to ride a bicycle. Lias Buzzacott is still a teasing joker, not yet the ardent suitor and picture of rectitude he will become in *Lias and Betty*. Sophie Grinnaway, the avid gossip known as the 'Muddlecombe Daily News', continues to spread misinformation around the parish when anything unusual occurs. Ned Annaferd (or Hannaford), the wheelwright — possibly based to some extent on the Puddington wheelwright and carpenter, Ned Knowles, in whose workshop Coles heard many anecdotes that he later turned into Jan Stewer stories — makes an occasional appearance, as does Tom Zalter, who has become a passenger in his own bus driven by his son. And of course Jan Stewer, when not telling of other characters' activities, makes fun of his own. Coles no doubt attributed to him some of his own characteristics, such as a mistrust of anything mechanical (motor vehicles above all; there is an irony in the fact that he died as a result of being knocked down by a lorry) and his lack of skill at games and handiwork. Jan's attempts to play cricket, football and golf are hilarious fiascos; when he tries to build a garden shed it is a botched job, and his paper hanging is as disastrous as in any music hall sketch.

The social hierarchy in Muddlecombe-in-the-Moor was unquestioned. The 'bettermos' volk' (always so designated by its inhabitants, apparently without irony) were the squire, the parson, the doctor and a few middle class persons with comfortable unearned incomes. Apart from the owners of the larger farms, the villagers are ordinary wage earners and their wives. The few very poor people tend to be women with large families or elderly widows. In general, women have the upper hand, or the last word, in domestic matters, and men are wary of doing anything to upset their wives.

Communal undertakings — usually set on foot by the 'bettermos' volk' — tend to cause ill feelings and disagreement, with comical results. Typical are 'The Jumble Sale' in *In Chimley Corner,* as well as 'The Whist Drive and Dance', in which Coles introduced another village, Excombe. One of its inhabitants tells Jan that they've had 'a Vancy Dress Ball. And what's more, us have had it bad. And what's furthermore still, 'twill be a gudish bit bevore us recovers from it'. The organiser had been a Miss Lucas, who is 'very good fer entertainments and sitch-like', having 'got up scores o' things to amuse the volks, sitch as missionary meetings and so forth.' In a two-part story, 'For the Good of the Cause' in *Yap,* Jan shows no enthusiasm for fund-raising events. 'The Cottage 'Ospital, that's a Cause, and the District Nurse is a Cause, and the Women's Sociable Union is a Cause; cause of more strife and bad-friendship in this parish than all the rest putt together. Church Expenses is a cause once a year, and so's Chapel Anniversity, and the Bell-ringers is a Cause when they'm jue to have a outin'. All the rest of the year they'm only a cause of annoyance.'

In an 'Author's Note' at the beginning of *A Parcel of Ol' Crams',* Coles said that this expression was one he loved. He suggested that the nearest English equivalent might be 'A pack of nonsense', but found this inadequate. He gave a number of instances of the use of the phrase, among them:

'A Labourer: They parleyment fellers don't know no more than my ole wumman's cat. I went to a meetin' and yeard one of 'em praich up a long ol' rigmarole vor dree parts of a hour, and 'twas a parcel of ol' crams from start to finish', and

Mrs A: What did you think of the lecsher in the Ins'ichute last night, Mrs B. about the calipsis of the mune, and the yarn about the earth gettin' in the light o' the zin and throwin' a shadow and makin' the mune go all black?'

Mrs B: A parcel of ol' crams, Mrs A.

Mrs A: My opinion zackly, Mrs B.'

Somewhat defensively, Coles added 'When my Muddlecombe neighbours see this book they will call it a "Parcel of ol' crams". So I have forestalled them.'

Mrs A's 'calipsis of the mune' is a reminder that Coles evidently gloried in the malapropisms he overheard or even, perhaps, sometimes invented. Did he really hear a Methodist hellfire preacher referred to as sankeymonious, or did he see how appropriate it would be? At a meeting of a debating society (a fiasco, as usual) there was 'no obliteration to spaik', and it was hoped that a proposal would be 'supported with animosity'. An architect might become an artichoke, spectacles, sparticles, there was a plan to install lectrisical light, an aerial was an airoyl, and Tom Zalter didn't mind being out in the rain because he was perfidious to damp. A series of lectures given by a doctor who 'come out yer twice a wik to larn us all about our innards' offered splendid opportunities: catterpillar's veins, compound fractions, infermation of the lungs and so on.

During the first thirty years of his writing life it evidently did not occur to Coles to provide glossaries when his stories, originally written for Devon readers of Devon newspapers, were published in book form — although he added a few definitions in the form of footnotes to some of the 'Carrier's Van' tales — orfis (eaves), blassid yet (blessed heat), zap (as it happens), tiddly (wren) and so on. However, when Herbert Jenkins decided to bring out the new edition of *Ole Biskit* in 1933, they may have suggested that non-Devonians would be puzzled by some of the words they came across. Accordingly Coles added a glossary of about 350 words 'for the better acquaintance of such as are unfamiliar with the Devon dialect'. Some are simply standard English spellings of dialect pronunciations (aigs, eggs; aishes, ashes; tay sassers, tea saucers; tayjis, tedious.) He prefaced his final collection of stories, *On the Moor of a Night,* published in 1949, with an 'Author's Apology' in which he said that the stories 'were not written with one eye on the Etymologist . . . They are intended merely for the general (and genial) reader who is willing, and therefore easy, to be entertained and amused. Consequently the text has not been strained, or circumstances created for the purpose of dragging in obscure dialect words or forms. On the contrary I have avoided archaic expressions rarely met with, being content with the language any visitor may hear any day in any Devon village. For the greater comfort of the ordinary reader I have also refrained from any extravagant attempts at phonetic spelling which hamper the "foreigner" without securing correct pronunciation. One realises that all this precludes any value as a work of reference; but as I have neither the skill nor the attainments to produce a work of that sort, no dignity so exalted has been contemplated for the present volume. It has, I am bound to confess, no loftier aim than to beguile an idle hour and perchance gladden the heart of, here and there, a West-country exile far from home.'

However it seems that when the book was published by the Westaway Press it was again thought desirable to add a glossary. Coles, tongue in cheek, appended 'a Few Observations by the Author on some of the less obvious words occurring in this Book, for the Greater Comfort of such Readers as may not have had the Privilege of a Devon Rustic Background or upbringing.' This contains only about half as many definitions as the previous one, but is interesting in that Coles took the opportunity to include notes on some of the dialect's specific features. For instance: 'ee (or y). Common terminations among our old folks for passive (sic) verbs. We milkee, pumpee, pickee. drinkee, walkee and grandfather's clock won't tickee'. and 'en: adjectival ending. We have a cripple man with a timbern leg who wears a cloathen coat with bonen buttons and a leathern belt. His garden has an oaken gate with stonen gateposts. His wife uses a tinnen kettle, a cloamen jug, a timbern spoon, and has a silvern thimble in a brassen box. Sometimes she brings home from the shop a boughten cake in a papern bag.'

The 1930s saw Coles succeeding not only as a writer and performer in the west country, but as a playwright. Even in his days as a schoolmaster in Puddington, he has taken an interest in amateur dramatics, and when he was teaching in Bovey Tracey he wrote a play called 'Revel Day' to be performed by some of the students he was teaching at evening classes. When they put it on in the village hall, it was greatly enjoyed by the audience, which included the Revd Sabine Baring Gould, rector of Lew Trenchard and immensely prolific author. Gould complimented Coles on his play, and told him that it should be taken further afield. In due course it was successfully performed at Newton Abbot, Exeter and Torquay. In 1922 it was revived in Torquay. Not long after this the whole Coles family formed themselves into a concert party, based themselves in rented rooms in Barnstaple, and toured towns and villages around the north of Devon.

During the next dozen years Cole wrote four more plays: 'The Cat and the Fiddle', 'Agatha's Heaven' and 'Barnet's Folly'. The first three all had local productions, but the fourth became the best known. As with much of Coles' work, the idea for this derived from a real happening. In 1927 he bought a farm near Exeter — probably at a knock-down price, as agriculture in Devon, as elsewhere, was in a depressed state between the wars. His son Colin managed it, and had the idea of organising a farming co-operative, but met with opposition. Such a scheme is the Barnet's Folly of the title. The play was first staged in Plymouth in 1931, put on in Torquay and Exeter soon afterwards, and eventually reached the Haymarket Theatre, London, in 1935, with Coles playing a leading part. His real name did not appear in programmes or on posters; Jan Stewer was given as both author and actor.

This was perhaps the high point of his career. The play was widely praised, toured the whole country, became a favourite with repertory and amateur companies, was broadcast and eventually presented on television.

Although he wrote no more plays, Coles continued to take a keen interest in the theatre, acting in and producing plays with amateur groups. During the Second World War he toured with CEMA, the Council for the Encouragement of Music and the Arts.

In his later years he wrote two full-length novels. The first of these, *Lias and Betty,* appeared in 1938. It is a romance, more or less a variation on the Cinderella story. Betty Urford, orphaned at the age of twelve, has been brought up by her aunt and uncle; taking the place of the Ugly Sisters, they expect her to work in the house and do their best to ensure that she has no social life or friends of either sex. Lias Buzzacott, too, is an orphan, regarded by many in the parish as a ne'er-do-well because he dresses like a tramp, is outspoken, takes nothing seriously and repeatedly changes jobs. Nevertheless he is incapable of telling a lie or breaking his word, is helpful to anyone in need and an excellent workman: in fact a prince among men. (The Lias Buzzacott who appeared in one or two earlier Jan Stewer stories was a far less idealised character.) In place of a fairy godmother are an elderly couple on whose farm Lias settles to work after he has fallen in love with Betty: they come to regard him as the son they never had and finally 'sell' their farm to him for half a crown, making it possible for him to marry Betty.

The second novel was *The Shop with Two Windows*, his last book, published when he was 76. It takes the form of a story narrated by Ned Annaford to 'our little party that rides into Exeter every market day' in Tom Zalter's bus, and originally appeared as a series of Jan Stewer's weekly stories. The shop of the title was founded in 1876 in Nackaburge, ('said to be Knockbridge on the map') by Seth Clampitt, son of a boozy village carrier, but himself by contrast a 'sankeymonious' Methodist preacher. His wife dies when their son Andy is only seven, and his younger sister Clara comes to keep house. She is as repressive and self-righteous as her brother, and even after Seth's death Andy, now in his late twenties, is allowed no say in the running of the shop or indeed his own life. Relief arrives when Aunt Clara has to spend some months in hospital after being knocked down by a car. Ned Hannaford persuades Andy to employ, as a temporary assistant, a bright, competent and confident girl, Bessie Kelland, who greatly improves the arrangement of the shop and attracts more custom. When Aunt Clara eventually returns, furious at the changes, Bessie manages to mollify her and even persuades her to accept that she and Andy intend to marry. This too, in a way, is a Cinderella story, though with a sex change — Andy's parents and Aunt Clara may be seen as the ugly sisters, while Bessie is in effect not only Fairy Godmother to Andy but also Princess Charming.

In a preface Coles said that readers of his earlier books would no doubt recognise that 'while still endeavouring to retain the idiom of the native language, I have modified to some extent the attempt to reproduce an exact phonetic rendering of the primitive dialect. I have done this with a view to making the story more easily readable for the many (including even some Devon urban dwellers) who are not familiar with the ancient vernacular of our more remote countryside.'

Both *The Shop with Two Windows* and *On the Moor of a Night* were published by the Westaway Press. This was a small imprint set up immediately after the Second World War by Waveney Girvan, who called himself an honorary Cornishman. An energetic man, qualified as a chartered accountant, he had worked for some years in Sheffield, where a steel firm manufactured a device he had invented, but with the end of the war he had been able to turn to his twin loves, books and the western counties. In the summer of 1946 he launched a new quarterly, the 'West Country Magazine', which published stories, poems and articles by such authors as Charles Causely, Eden Philpotts and the theatre critic J.C. Trewin, as well as other lesser-known writers. In addition, he founded the West Country Writers' Association , which held its first Congress at Bath in 1951 (and still flourishes). Eden Philpotts was its first president and A.J. Coles was one of its eleven vice-presidents. Others included Christopher Fry, A.L. Rowse and Henry Williamson. (When Philpotts died in 1950, Williamson succeeded him as president, but resigned after five years and returned to being a vice-president.)

Girvan evidently knew and admired Coles' work, and not only published his last two books, but took over the four brought out by Herbert Jenkins in the 1920s and 1930s: *Ole Biskit, In Chimley Corner, Yap* and *A Parcel of ol' Crams*. They were advertised on the back covers of several issues of the 'West Country Magazine' among other Westaway Books.

Royalties from the reissues of this earlier work must have been welcome to Coles as, after an astonishing writing career of more than fifty years, he found his creativity failing. In 1951 he and his wife moved to the village of Tedburn St Mary, not far from the farm out of which the idea for 'Barnet's Folly' had grown. They celebrated their diamond wedding there ten years later; his wife died not long afterwards (she was five years older than her husband). Coles lived for another four years, remaining in good health. His death was sudden: while staying with friends in Dorset, he went out for a walk alone and, as has been said, was struck and killed by a lorry.

In the autumn of 1949 Coles contributed an article, 'This Dreadful Dialect', to the 'West Country Magazine', It began:

'Some years ago a teacher at a remote Devon village school enquired in despairing tones, "What can one do to cure the children of this dreadful dialect?"

I replied. "Not very much, thank goodness. It is not dreadful and it shouldn't be cured."

"Only endured?"

"No. Taught. Moreover." I added. "it should be a punishable offence for any teacher to give the children cause to suppose that the native speech of their forefathers is something to be regretted. On the contrary, they should be led to perceive how much in it.is dignified, beautiful, historic and romantic. To this end, all teachers should be examined in their proficiency in the dialect of their own district." '

He went on to recall the way 'fifty years ago I was teaching quite a few rustic youngsters to speak moderately good English (as that term is popularly understood) by using the dialect as a foundation.' He gave examples of his method.

'Teacher: Greet me in good Devon, enquiring after my health.

Class: Gude morning, how be yu (alternatively how be getting vore; knacking along?)

Teacher: Now the same in King's English.

Class: Good morning, how are you (getting on: progressing?)

Teacher: Willie Webber, translate into Devon "Where are you going with that great stump of a tree?

Willie: Where be gwaine wi' thikky gurt moot?

Here follows a roar of laughter, and let me say at once that a teacher who does not know how to use laughter should leave this method alone — and teaching. Willie must be complimented on having done pretty well.'

Coles liked to lead his children to a realisation that 'what is now labelled "dialect" was once current English used by the best people,' and that a word such as 'suant' might be found in the early edition of Webster's Dictionary. Sometimes he would say a phrase in dialect and see how quickly the children could 'translate' it. (Where be to? Let'n bide where he's to. Be gwaine or no? He done it hissel'. You'm proper mazed.) Alternatively, he would ask the children to supply the dialect version of standard English phrases (We caught a mole: Us ketched a want; Close that door and latch it, Put vast thikky door and 'apse 'n; Tom and I will teach you. Me and Tom'll larn'ee)

English lessons with Mr Coles must have been fun.

Apart from a few years at a village school and, presumably, a spell at a teachers' training college, Coles was self-educated. His wit, energy and creativity enabled him to become the supreme interpreter of that 'ancient vernacular' to which he was devoted. Lively and often wonderfully funny, his stories provide, in vocabulary, grammar, idiom and, phonetically reproduced, a record of the Devon dialect in print that has never been surpassed. A superb natural humorist, a shrewd observer of his fellows and a Devonian of Devonians, he was outstanding in his knowledge of his county, its people and the 'native speech of their forefathers'.

Chapter Ten

The 1920's: Henry Williamson's *The Village Book* and *The Labouring Life*

The annual get-togethers of the West Country Writers' Association, known officially as Congresses, were held at many different towns and cities in the western counties — Plymouth, Bristol, Weymouth, Barnstaple, Truro and others. Both A.J. Coles and Henry Williamson attended frequently. Presumably they sometimes met and talked, especially on convivial evenings in the bar of whatever hotel the Association had chosen. Possibly they had read one another's work. In background, upbringing and temperament they were dissimilar, and although both had served in the First World War, Williamson, the younger by nineteen years, had seen action on the Western Front whereas Coles, as has been said, remained, through no fault of his own, in a non-combatant unit. Yet they were alike in one important respect, that influenced them both as writers: they were devoted to Devon and took pleasure in the speech of its people.

Williamson was born in 1895 in Brockley, in the borough of Lewisham, then still part of Kent, and it was in the woods and fields of Kent that he first developed a love of natural history, and especially birds. In May, 1914, as a youth of eighteen, he spent a fortnight's holiday from the job in a London insurance firm he had begun during the previous summer after leaving school. A spinster sister of his father had rented a cottage in Georgeham. She invited him to stay there. He was at once enraptured with the countryside and the long sand beaches and dunes of the north-west of Devon. It was the beginning of a life-long love of the county in which he was to spend, in all, some forty-eight years of his life. In March, 1921, after a quarrel with his father, he rode his Norton motorbike to Georgeham and settled down to live and write in a rented cottage. He had a small disability pension from the army, having served for five years. He was already a writer; his first novel, *The Beautiful Years,* had been accepted and would be published that autumn. He was confident that he could earn his living by writing, and was to prove himself right.

Living in Georgeham seemed to stimulate him to a period of intense creativity. By the end of the 1920s he was the author of eight published books. In addition to four autobiographical novels to which he gave the overall title *The Flax of Dream* there were three collections of nature stories — *The Lone Swallows, The Peregrine Saga* and *The Old Stag* — and the book which would establish his reputation and would always be identified with him as though he had written nothing else, *Tarka the Otter*.

During his early years in Georgeham he spent many evenings in one or other of the two pubs, the Rock or the Kings Arms, known as the Higher House and the Lower House, listening to the talk that provided him with material for articles and stories that he could sell to newspapers and magazines. 'In the Higher House and the Lower House I heard many tales of falcons, foxes, badgers, ravens, men, which afterwards I wrote as stories,' he recalled in a collection of some of them published by Jonathan Cape in 1930 under the title *The Village Book*. Two years later he followed this with *The Labouring Life*.

Anxious, perhaps, that his neighbours would recognise themselves in his stories and feel resentful, Williamson prefaced *The Village Book* with a disclaimer, calling it 'an imaginative work which should not be read as the history of any particular village, and certainly not of any man or woman. Even the "I" and "zur" and the "Mr Williamson" of certain pages . . . are but devices of story telling.' However, in his preface to the American edition of *The Labouring Life*, he admitted that the characters were based on living people, although he accused himself, perhaps justly, of manipulating them, transforming them into Williamson characters for the purposes of fiction. Nevertheless the people of the villages of Georgeham and Croyde, their way of life, their ideas and beliefs, as well as their patterns of speech, ring true. The two books offer a fragment of social history and a convincing picture of a remote parish before it became a popular holiday place and the building of hundreds of houses to be occupied by incomers engulfed it.

Williamson had grown up to the sound of south-east London voices, but his ears were quickly attuned to the slower, gentler speech of Devon. It fascinated him. At a 'rabbit supper', given by Charlie Ovey, who had recently taken over the Kings Arms, he talked to one of the men who in those days were employed to break up stones for road-making, who spoke 'good and simple English; some of his phrases, the plain common phrases of the country, I wrote down in my notebook at the time, and later was astonished, and delighted, to find the same phrase in Shakespeare. (He had not taken them down from the book Shakespeare, but the living Shakespeare had taken them from common speech.) Sometimes in talk, when meeting a friend in the lanes, I would ask for a phrase to be repeated; and almost invariably the speaker would hesitate, deprecate his own language, and explain. "That's how us says it, the rough way, you know; it ban't the educated way of saying it, no doubt." Also with what is called dialect words — they hid them sometimes from strangers, believing them to be inferior; some of them probably in English use before the Norman conquest, others as old. Fitchy (stoat), dreshel (flail) weest (dreary), dimmity (twilight). He was as proper man as ever trod ground. Wait until the ground's in temper (i.e. the garden soil warm and loose from digging); it's no good mucketting. The exact and simple speech of their forefathers, until they understood I was finding value in it, was deprecated.'

In the cottage he first occupied his next-door neighbour was known as Revvy because at one time he had worked at the Rectory. He and his small son Ernie were soon contributing words and phrases to the writer's notebook. Referring to the barn owls that nested in the rafter space above the cottage ceiling, he told Williamson 'I like vor hear they oyls up auver' and his son chimed in excitedly, 'I zeed, I zeed a master girt oyl looking out of your dark hole, mister! Last night, I did. Yass!' Revvy's wife, like many of the villagers, quickly decided that the writer was 'mazed as a brish' or 'winnicky', and remarked that his garden was a 'passle-ole-crawsclawsmores'.

Williamson learned that a small boy was a little tacker, and a boy or youth who behaved wildly might be known as a young heller. The valerian growing on cottage walls was called drunkards, thistles in gardens and fields were milky dashels, and couch grass was stroyle. The passageway outside his cottage was a drang, a small cleave or valley was a goyal, and a field headland was a vorridge (fore-hedge). A farmer told him that when ploughing he couldn't go wrong: 'So long as I could zee a stick in the vorridge, I'd drive straight to'n, straight as a gun-shot.' On a spring day a holm-scritch or grey-thrush — a mistlethrush — would sing in the churchyard elms, and when he walked down the valley towards Croyde and stopped to speak to Grannie Parsons, who lived in the smallest cottage in the parish, she told him 'tes proper weather, midear, 'tes butiful weather, and the l'il grass-bird be back by the stream', so that he knew that the chiffchaff had returned from migration. And less happily there was John Kift, who boasted of shooting ackymals. 'Every wan I zee near my pays! I load me gun with a half-charge, and blow ivry wan of the l'il beggars abroad. Seventy-eight I've shute this year, and in the spring my son blocked up half-a-dozen nesties in holes in walls roundabout . . . yes, zur! And if us didden do that, us wouldn't have a pay left, noomye!' Williamson protested that tomtits ate insects on the peas not the peas themselves, but Kift insisted that they ate peas as well. 'They be master birds for pays, the rogues! But this one won't ate no more pays'. He took the writer to see his rows of peas. 'Knack, knack, knack, the l'il hellers go on them, and I'll shute ivry wan I see!'

Williamson noted that four different kinds of titmice were lying on the ground — great, blue, coal and marsh — and knew that marsh tits, at least, did not eat peas. However, he was unable to persuade the gun-happy gardener of this, just as he was unable to persuade the London-born wife of villagers that a slow-worm, called a longcripple's mate (a longcripple being a viper) is a harmless lizard. Having left it beside the wall of a neighbouring barn, he found it dead on his return, 'broken and battered by stones.'

Williamson enjoyed listening to old men whose memories went well back into Victorian times. There was the owner of a barn adjoining the larger cottage to which he moved after his marriage in 1925, who told him ' 'Twas a dancing barn when I was a boy. Many's the time I've a-zin young men and maids a-dancing in this yurr barn by lantern light. And it was proper dancing in they days, too.' When the writer noticed a hollow in the limeash floor he was told, 'Now that was done by my father and his father avore'n, beating out corn with a dreshel. I've a-zin my father knacking all night, when I was a boy. Twadden like today, you know, they was hard times, and no mistake . . . My dear soul, I've a-zin men in the harvest field working fifteen or sixteen hours straight off, and the vrost showing though their leather belts the whole time, as they stooped behind the reaper to bind the sheaves! and get one shilling and threepence for it!' When Williamson queried the word 'vrost'. he was told, 'Well, that's what us calls it hereabouts. 'Twas so hot, you see, that a man would sweat all the time. Yes, there was beer, for those that wanted it, but it twadden all who might want beer. 'Twas small ale, and likely to give a man the guts-ache. Some used to like it, no doubt. My dear soul, men used to sweat when they worked in they days: tidden so today.' He complained that an employer had to pay a labouring man one pound, twelve shillings and sixpence a week. 'And what do we get for it? Why, if it rains, they'm oomwards!'

However, the owner of the barn was no employer of labour; he owned a few acres and two cows; a bachelor, he lived at home with his aged mother.

The oldest man in the parish was Jacob Ley, known as Sparker, who spoke 'a slow and beautiful dialect, the broadest I ever heard. He had been a noted wrestler at one time, and had won the championship at the annual Georgeham Revel year after year. The parson in those days, one of the family named Hole, members of which were rectors of Georgeham from 1783 to 1871, with only one three-year break, gave the men a pint of ale before wrestling began to 'put them all in proper temper. Pass'n's man did boil thiccy malt, that was the tithe barley of Varmer Brown, of Crowcombe, that growed the best malting barley i' th' parish. Pass'n's man was as proper a man for brewing as ever broke a bit of bread. 'Twas zaid one time when a' opened the zack o' malt that a master girt rat zat there scrupering and chittering, and pass'n's man tipped rat and malt into vurnace together. 'Twas master ale from his reverenz' barrels, aiy! master stuff. 'Twould spring in flame out of the vire when you drowed a spoonful on the hearth.'

(Williamson explains that it was 'the custom of the wrestling champion to spill on his hearth, for luck, a spoonful of the winner's ale brought home in his gallon firkin, or wooden keg.' A remarkable ale indeed that would flame as though it was brandy.)

Although Williamson called himself 'the serious historian of the village' at the end of the chapter called 'Devonshire Cider' in *Life in a Devon Village,* he was simply the chronicler of eight years of its life in the 1920s. His two books written at the end of the decade offer impressions of some three dozen of its inhabitants — men, women and children; children, especially, amused and sometimes exasperated him. Such small happenings as the cutting down of the churchyard elms, and the death of a cow followed by that of its aged owner become, in his vivid and sympathetic accounts, dramatic events. Like Coles, he took a satirical view of parish politics, but whereas Coles only sought to provide his readers with an amusing story, Williamson's purpose, in this respect, was indeed more serious. Any communal activities or discussions were usually instigated by the rector and various middle-class residents — retired army and navy officers and persons living on unearned incomes (Coles' phrase 'bettermos' volk' for such people does not seem to have been used in Georgeham). The village had no squire, although Col. Elliott, who owned Pickwell Manor, a mile away, may have been regarded as filling that position. (He was influential in ensuring that in 1926 Georgeham acquired a building then always referred to as the Village Institute, as Muddlecombe's was the 'Ins'ichute') As parish councillors the rector, the Revd Alfred Rose, Col. Elliott and Captain Bigge, R.N., retired, were all concerned with long series of acrimonious discussions, covering four years, to which Williamson devoted perhaps rather too much space — more than fifty pages — of *The Labouring Life* under the title 'Cemetery or Burial Ground?' which had the ironic title 'A Democratic Story'. It contains little dialect, but the landlord of the Kings Arms, called Charlie Taylor (in real life Charlie Ovey) is given a short speech more or less summing up village opinion: 'What do you boogers do, tho'? You'm all talk, talk, meanwhile us be gettin' older and older and soon us'll all be stiff as gurnets, and nowhere to be put when us be gone. Talkin' never got a man nowhere, you'm all alike, clitter clatter and flim-flam, dravin' away like a proper ole local praicher, like the wind you be, and saying "disgraceful", "Should be stopped", "Where be the Country comin' to?" "Tidden like it was in my young days!" — Bah! if I'd my way I'd drown the lot of you like a litter of kittens.'

As the extracts quoted show, Williamson was sparing with the phonetic spelling of dialect words. Unlike Coles, he was writing, from the beginning, in the hope of acceptance by London editors and publishers who might be wary of offering their readers too unfamiliar a dialect. He found that even the modest number of Devon dialect words in *Tarka* could arouse objections from reviewers. He included in *The Labouring Life* (but omitted from *Life in a Devon Village*) a chapter headed 'Provincialism', saying that it was the substance of a letter written to John (later Sir John) Squire, the Plymouth-born poet and literary journalist who was editor of 'The London Mercury', a magazine he had established in 1919. A reviewer had complained that the book showed an excessive use of provincialisms and sporting jargon. Williamson took the words objected to one at a time, providing definitions. They included channered, belving, shillets. vuz-peg, pollywiggles, ruddock, cracky, aerymouse, appledrane, brock, vair, fitchey, tacker and clitter. He added that one of his reasons for using such words was 'to preserve them before they pass away. The daily newspapers are making a stereotyped speech in rural England; even the middle-aged men are a little shy of their natural speech, while only the naughtiest of the village children sometimes talk as their forefathers talked, as when Shakespeare was alive and listening.' He finished by saying, 'Well, my dear Jack Squire, I — a mere immigrant — most sincerely hope that in *The Labouring Life* and its fellow *Village Book,* I have not despoiled your native Devon. If I have, it is because of a defect which I do not know how to repair; for I wish, were I dying, to sleep in its dear soil,' (His wish was granted when he died in 1977; his grave is in the old part of Georgeham churchyard.)

In 1929 he left Georgeham for sixteen years, although he quite often returned on visits, usually staying in the hut on the hill to the north-east of the village he had bought following the success of *Tarka.* He spent the last eight of those years struggling to restore the fertility of a run-down farm in north Norfolk. In 1945, after his first marriage had come to an end, he sold the farm and returned to his little hilltop hut. In that year Faber took over from Jonathan Cape *The Village Book* and *The Labouring Life*; this gave Williamson the opportunity to revise and rearrange them, and they appeared as *Life in a Devon Village* and *Tales of a Devon Village,* with much of the original nature writing excised.

Williamson and Coles, two dissimilar writers who happened to be near contemporaries, both left a considerable body of work produced during writing lives of more than fifty years — yet for both, their books of the 1920s happen to be those by which they are best remembered. The Devonian by descent and the Devonian by adoption each made a distinctive contribution to that long record of Devon dialect in print which has become part of the history of the county.

Four Centuries of Devon Dialect

as recorded in print

Notes

Chapter One

1. C.F. Tucker Brooke, in his introduction to *The Apocryphal Shakespeare,* suggests that Shakespeare may have cooperated in some of the doubtful plays as reviser or elaborator, and that 'During his long and many-sided connection with the stage, the poet-manager would doubtless have had occasion to retouch and refine much of the inferior work that came to his company.'
2. Michael Justin Davis, *The Landscape of William Shakespeare.* Webb and Bower/Michael Joseph, 1987.

Chapter Two

1. John Cock, *Records of the Antient (sic) Borough of South Molton.* Published privately. 1893.
2.Derek Hudson, *Sir Joshua Reynolds, a Personal Study.* Geoffrey Bles, 1958.

Chapter Three

1. *Dictionary of National Biography;* Tom Girtin, *Doctor with Two Aunts,* Hutchinson, 1959.
2. W. Kearley Wright, *West Country Poets, their Lives and Work. London, 1896*
3. W. Kearley Wright. op. cit
4. W.J.R. Aggett, *The Bloody Eleventh:* History of the Devonshire Regiment, Vol. II, 1815-1914. Published by the Devonshire and Dorset Regiment, 1995.

Chapter Five

1.Hilda Walker, 'History of the Devonshire Association, 1862-1962'. Devonshire Association Transactions Vol. 94, pp 42-106.

Chapter Six

1. Arthur Wilde, 'Dartmoor Home of Writer'. 'Express and Echo', October 2nd, 1959.

Chapter Seven

1. Richard Pearse Chope: 'Devon Dialect Letter', Devonshire Association

Transactions, Vol. 45, pp 276-301

'The Book Dialect of North Devon', DAT Vol. 49. 'Devon Plant Names', DAT Vol. 64, pp. 325-77. 'Devon Bird Names', DAT Vol. 65, pp. 257-92. 'Devon Fish Names', DAT Vol. 67, pp. 421-53. Obituary of Richard Chope, DAT Vol. 79.

Bibliography

Henry Baird, *Nathan Hogg's Letters to es Brither Jan.* London, 1847; second edition, 1850. New series, including 'Mucksy Lane', 1863

Revd Sabine Baring-Gould, *Songs and Ballads of the West.* Methuen, 1892

C.F. Tucking Brooke, *The Shakespeare Apocrypha.* Oxford University Press, 1918

Douglas Cock, *Jan Stewer, a West Country Biography,* Moonraker Press, 1980

A.J. Coles, (Jan Stewer):*Zum vunny Demshur Tellins.* No date: c. 1904

Jan Stewer's Demshur Buke. No date; perhaps 1905

Jan Stewer at Home and Abroad, c. 1922

Ole Biskit, Besley and Copp, Exeter, 1915. Republished by Herbert Jenkins, 1933; Westaway Books, 1948; Alan Sutton, 1987

In Chimley Corner, Herbert Jenkins, 1937; Westaway Books, c. 1950; Alan Sutton, 1980

A Parcel of Ol' Crams, Herbert Jenkins, 1930; Westaway Books, c. 1950; Alan Sutton, 1980

Yap, Herbert Jenkins, 1938; Westaway Books, c. 1951; Alan Sutton, 1987

Lias and Betty, Herbert Jenkins, 1938; Westaway Books

On the Moor of a Night, Westaway Books, 1949

The Shop with Two Windows, Westaway Books, 1952

H.J. Daniel, *A Companion to the Cornish Thalia.* (Contains 'Roger and Patty, an eclogue in the Devon Dialect') Published privately

Michael Justin Davis, *The Landscape of William Shakespeare,* Webb and Bower/ Michael Joseph, 1987

Frederic Elworthy, editor: *The Exmoor Scolding and Courtship:* two dialogues of the beginning of the 18th century, with a complete transcript in Glossic, the vocabulary enlarged and the whole illustrated with copious notes. Bungay, 1879. *The West Somerset Word Book,* a Glossary of Archaic Words and Phrases used in the West of Somerset and East Devon. The English Dialect Society, London, 1886

Sir John Fortescue *The Story of a Red Deer,* Macmillan, 1897

Tom Girtin, *Doctor with Two Aunts,* Hutchinson,1959

Revd W. Gregory Harris, *Sketches of the West Countree, Down-along-o'-We, Zummerset Volk and Devonshire Diversions, West Country Volk, John Lane, 1923*

William Hazlitt, *The Doubtful Plays of Shakespeare*. Routledge, London, no date.

Sarah Hewett, *The Peasant Speech of Devon*. London, 1892

Nummits and Crummits. London, 1894

Derek Hudson, *Sir Joshua Reynolds, a Personal Study*. Geoffrey Bles, 1958

William Marshall, *Rural Economy of the West of England*, 1796

Revd Thomas Moore, *History of Devonshire from the Earliest Period to the Present*, London, 1829

Hannah O'Neill, *Devonshire Idyls*. Third edition, Exeter and London, 1892

Mary Palmer, *Devonshire Dialogues*. Published privately by her daughter, Mrs Gwatkin, 1839

W.S. Pasmore, *Tales of Devon and Cornwall*. Third edition, Exeter, 1900

George Pulman *Rustic Sketches*, 1842. Third edition, London, 1871

William Rock, *Jim and Nell*. London, 1867

E. Cruwys Sharland, *Ways and Means in a Devonshire Village*. SPCK, 1885

F.J. Snell, *A Book of Exmoor*, Methuen, 1903

Cecil Torr, *Small Talk at Wreyland*, Cambridge University Press, 1926

William Weeks, *Bits o' Broad Devon*. Second edition, Exeter, 1902; fifth edition, Exeter and London, 1924. *Devonshire Yarns*. Second edition, Exeter, 1907. New edition, greatly enlarged, Exeter, 1926. *'Twas Ordained, Exeter, 1921*

Henry Williamson *The Village Book*, Jonathan Cape, 1930: *The Labouring Life*, Jonathan Cape, 1932. Revised editions of these two books were published by Faber in 1945 under the titles *Tales of a Devon Village* and *Life in a Devon Village*.

John Wolcot, (Peter Pindar) *Poems*.

R.N. Worth, *West Country Garland*, London, 1875

Joseph Wright, editor: *The English Dialect Dictionary*. Putnam, London, Six volumes 1898-1905

W.H. Kearley Wright, *West Country Poets, their Lives and Works*. London, 1896

Appendix One

Before the advent of the tape recorder, writers could only convey an idea of the sound of any dialect by the use of phonetics, and before the advent of universal education, those who knew a dialect best were unlikely to be literate enough to attempt this, or indeed to feel that the way they spoke was worthy of record — an attitude that Henry Williamson noted in Georgeham as recently as the 1920s. Also, until around the beginning of the 19th century, not many of those who had the advantage of education seem to have taken much interest in what the upper classes tended to consider crude, uncouth and boorish ways of speech.

For all that, in Devon, examples of the work of writers who evidently appreciated the county's dialect, or dialects — since vocabulary and pronunciation inevitably varied from district to district — survive in increasing numbers from the early 17th century and on through the 18th and 19th centuries and into the 20th.

Once examples of Devon dialect began to appear in publications with a national distribution, it became desirable for them to be provided with glossaries. It is not surprising that the contributor who sent a copy of the 'Exmoor Scolding' to the 'Gentleman's Magazine' in 1746, and seemingly was not a Devonian, asked readers to send in definitions of the many dialect words. Of the writers whose work is mentioned in this book, two, Hannah O'Neill and Henry Williamson, used dialect words sparingly and usually left their meaning to be gathered from their context. Others merely added word lists for the information of their readers. William Marshall included 320 'provincialisms of West Devonshire' in his *Rural Economy of the West of England* (1796). The Rev. Thomas Moore, in Book IV of his *History of Devonshire* (1839) gave 'A List of some of the Provincialisms formerly at least prevalent, chiefly among the Common People of the County, though now probably, from the influence of modern improvements, gradually getting out of Use'. More elaborate glossaries were Frederic Elworthy's to the 'Exmoor Scolding' and 'Exmoor Courtship'; John Palmer's to his grandmother's 'Devonshire Dialogues' (which has been chosen here in preference to that prepared for Mrs Palmer by the Rev. Phillips); Sophia Hare's to a dialect letter written by an anonymous 'South Devon Lady' (possibly Sophia herself) found by W.K. Knight among old papers and submitted by Richard Chope to the Devonshire Association's Transactions in 1913; William Rock's to his verse playlet 'Jim and Nell' (1867); Miss S.P. Fox's given as an appendix to her *Kingsbridge and its Surroundings* (1874); Sarah Hewett's in her *The Peasant Speech of Devon;* and A.J. Coles' (Jan Stewer's) to his last two novels, *On the Moor of a Night* and *The Shop with Two Windows.*

That by no means all the words included in these publications are exclusive to Devon is shown by a look through the English Dialect

Dictionary. This valuable work, founded on the publications of the English Dialect Society, was edited and published at his own expense by Joseph Wright, professor of comparative philology at Oxford University. He brought out the first volume, A - C, in 1898; the sixth and last appeared in 1905. He expressed his gratitude for a bequest and a grant from the Royal Bounty. 'Had it not been for this timely substantial support, the labours of hundreds of people, extending over nearly a quarter of a century, would have been spent in vain; for I had exhausted all my own money, mounting to considerably over £2,000'. He dedicated the dictionary to the Rev. Professor W.W. Skeat, founder and president of the English Dialect Society: 'The unwearied worker in the varied field of English scholarship, to whose patient industry and contagious enthusiasm in connection with the laborious task of accumulating dialect material, the possibility of compiling an adequate Dictionary of English Dialect is mainly due'.

It was said to be 'the complete vocabulary of all dialect words still in use, or known to have been in use, during the last two hundred years.' It included lists of voluntary readers (about 350), unprinted collections of dialect words (about 330) and of correspondents. The names of Frederic Elworthy and Richard Pearse Chope appear in all three; that of Sarah Hewett (then given as 'of Torquay') in the second and third.

The Dictionary shows the wide distribution of some words. 'Arrish', for stubble, for instance, was found in the dialects of all the counties of southern England, including the Isle of Wight. The mud and straw building material, cob, occurred in East Anglia, Hampshire, Dorset and Cornwall. 'Beat', to pare turf off the ground for burning, to which Devon gave the word 'Denshiring', occurred in that sense in Shropshire, Herefordshire, Radnor, Montgomeryshire and Cornwall. 'Clavel', the chimneypiece or cross-beam of a hearth, was to be found in Herefordshire, Gloucester, Wiltshire, Dorset, Somerset and Cornwall, and 'cruel', in the sense of 'very', in Cumberland, Lancashire, Cheshire, Warwickshire, Oxford, Dorset and Somerset. Devon shared many more words with other counties, and even in some instances with Ireland and Scotland.

To return to individual glossaries, William Rock included a number of words which were evidently in nationwide use in his day, and remain so, as: gaff, heft, horseplay, huggermugger, lissom, lopsided, pudgy, rubble, slapdash, squash, squeal and swathe, among others. These have been omitted, as well as spellings which simply represent Devon speakers' pronunciation of familiar words. Sarah Hewett, for example, has 'asiniate' for assassinate, 'awpels' for apples, 'baynes' for beans, 'ekal' for equal, 'herzel' for herself. 'tosticated' for intoxicated, 'saysan' for season and others. Also, with a few exceptions, if a word appears in only one writer's glossary it is not included here.

For the glossary that follows, nothing can be claimed except that it is a personal selection of words which seem of particular interest.

Abbreviations are:
FE: Frederic Elworthy
JP: James Palmer
WM: William Marshall
TM: The Rev. Thomas Moore
RC: Richard Chope
WR:William Rock
MF: Miss Fox
ON: Hannah O'Neill
SH: Sarah Hewett
JS: Jan Stewer (A.J. Coles)
HW: Henry Williamson
DA: Devonshire Association's reports on dialect in the annual volumes of Transactions, 1877-1998 (until 1963 always referred to as 'Verbal provincialisms').

A

Abroad, all abroad, open, TM, RC. Split open, SH. '"Took 'n abroad", took it to pieces. If a person has falled abroad he has got fat': JS.

Ackmal, ackymal, with many variations including hackmaul,heckmal and hickymal, JP, WR, MF, SH, HW and DA 1887. Usually refers to blue tits and great tits but WR identified 'ackmal' as a nuthatch.

Aerymouse, a bat, HW. See 'sheerymouse'.

Agest, afraid, terrified, FE, TM.

Agenst, agin, aginst, to go to meet someone, RC, SH, JS. DA 1879, 1884 and 1910.

Agging, egging on or provoking, FE, WR: 'egging on or raising quarrels'

Akether, quoth he, forsooth, JP, WR.

Alkitotle, 'a silly oaf or foolish Elf', FE, WR.

All mops and brooms, drunk, DA 1877.

Allernbatch, an old sore, FE, JP, WR.

All-of-a-hu-u-u, all awry, SH. All of a huh, used by JS in *Ole Biskit;* all-a heh, DA1925, all of a diz, DA1932; all of a whurraw, DA 1936.

'Amlet' (Hamlet) JS says that 'To play 'Amlet is to create a scene with great show of feeling'. His car, *Ole Biskit*, would 'spit and cough and play 'Amlet'.

Ammil, hoar frost when it settles on trees and shrubs, SH. DA 1961, 'a layer of ice that forms on wires, stubble, twigs, etc., in certain weather.'

Ampassy, ampersand, JP, SH.

Aneest, near, FE, TM, DA 1900.

Anglebowing, a kind of fencing against sheep, FE, JP.

Angledog, an earthworm, DA 1889.

Angletwitch, an earthworm, JP, WR, DA 1895 and 1931.

Appledrane, a wasp, WM, MF, SH, JS, DA 1911.

Aprilled, sour, FE, JP, TM, WR.

Aps or apse, an abscess, RC, MF, DA 1884.

Apurt, sullen, FE, JP, TM, WR.

Aquott, a-quatt, weary of eating, WR: see also quat, quott.

Arrant, errand, FE, JP. JS says the best definition of 'arrants' is perhaps 'the articles which form the object of an errand, rarely used in the singular to denote the journey itself'. He used it in this sense in his stories, as did ON and others.

Arrish, arrishes, stubble, stubble field, JP, TM, MF, SH. ON: 'harrishes, earidges'. DA 1929.

Arrish mows, field stacklets. TM,WR, DA 1962.

Ashwaddle: JP has this simply as 'waddle', and WR has 'a waddling, unwieldy woman', but FE claims that 'an ashpadder or pedlar' collected dry ashes from farm house, and points out that wood ash was then used to make lye, used in place of soap.

Asneger, an ass, WR.

Athert or athurt, crosswise, athwart, FE, RC, SH. DA 1935 has simply 'athwart' but DA 1939 has 'wary, askew'.

Ausney, to anticipate bad news, TM. WR: 'to augur, to anticipate'. DA 1938 defines it as 'to predict, foretell, divine, conjecture . . . This is really 'halseny,' and really means to divine with a halse or halze rod'.

Auvis, eaves of a building, DA 1949: see 'oavis'.

Avroar or avrore, frosty, frozen, FE, JP, TM, RC, WR.

Away-do-go, off he went, spoken as one word implies departing at speed, JS. DA 1929 gives the same definition.

B.

B from a bull's foot: not to know B from a bull's foot was to be stupid or ignorant, DA 1882.

Backsevore, backsivore, back to front, WR, SH, JS, DA 1910. DA 1886: 'backanvore',

Baggage, for a woman, but baggaged, be-hagged or bewitched, FE. WR: begayged; JS: begaged.

Baisire, auricula, WR, DA 1885. DA 1931 gives 'basher' as an alternative pronunciation and suggests that the original name was 'bear's ear'.

Bandy, a game like that of golf, JP.

Banes, banns, FE.

Banging, large, great, FE, SH (also 'banging-gert').

Barngun, shingles, FE and DA 1931. JP: 'an eruption of pimples on trunk'.

Barker, a whetstone, WM, TM, WR, MF. DA 1953: 'baulker, cigar-shaped stone used to whet such implements as scythes'.

Barm, yeast, WR, SH. Spelled 'bourm' by FE.

Barra, a gilt pig, FE, WR, SH.

Barraquail, prevents traces from touching horses' heels, WR.

Bassam or bissam, heath, JP. TM has besom or bizzom. WM gives its Latin name as *Spartium Scoparium,* which suggests that he thought it to be a member of the broom family rather than heather. DA 1928 has 'bassomy, of a deep bronze-purple colour'. The word 'besom' is derived from bassam, as brooms were made from it.

Baste, to beat thoroughly, FE and SH. (JP has bace or bumbaste).

Bate, to quarrel, FE, WR.

Beat, bate, peat or turf, WM. TM: 'the roots and soil subjected to the operation of "burning beat"'. A beating axe was used for this. JP. gives a more detailed description: 'Beat or burning beat (Denshiring): ploughing or digging up turves, drying them and burning them before returning them to soil'. WR only gives 'peat or turf'. DA 1910 and 1964 give accounts of this practise, recorded as early as 1775 in Ash's Dictionary.

Bed-ale: FE says this was brewed for a gossiping or christening feast, and quotes Brand's *Popular Antiquities* as giving 'Bride-ales, church-ales, clerk-ales, give-ales, lamb-ales, leet-ales, Midsummer-ales, Scot-ales, Whitsun-ales and several more'. WR: 'ale brewed for conviviality at a birth'.

Been, a withy, band or twisted twig: TM, WM, WR. SH: 'beam or beem, a binder'. DA 1881.

Bedlier, an invalid, SH, ON. JS: 'bed-layer'. DA 1885 and 1916.

Begaged, begayged, bewitched, JP, WR. (see 'baggage').

Begoodged, bedevilled, WR (and see 'By Goodger').

Bellyharm, colic, WR.

Belve, to bellow, WR, MF, HW and JS, who gives the definition 'low, the song of a cow'. DA 1915 and 1963

Ben, to the true ben or bend, soundly and to the purpose, FE, JP, WR.

Bettermost, superior, JP; best, WR; of a higher social class, SH; upperclass, JS, who said he 'once heard an old man divide the community into "they that is worth thousands, and they that is worthwhile"'. DA 1910, DA 1971.

Betwit, to upbraid, TM, WR.

Bewattled: FE says this means 'seized with a fit of tattling, or betotled and turned fool'. JP: 'betwatted, besotted with stupidity'.

Bibble, to drink, to tipple, WR.

Biddle, JS: see 'bittle'.

Bigative, conceited, JS. DA 1914.

Billers, cow parsley. DA 1905 and 1920 give this as *Heracleum sphondyllum,* which is in fact hogweed.

Bisgee or bizgie, a tubal or twobill: see 'twobill'. DA 1889 gives this as phyzgie, a pickaxe.

Bittle, a large wooden hammer or mallet, WR, SH (the latter spells it 'bittel').

Bittle-headed, stupid. Sir John Fortescue uses this in *The Story of a Red Deer,* and JS has 'biddle 'aid'.

Biver, to shake, shiver or quiver, TM, WR, MF, SH, JS. SH illustrated the word with a pathetic story of a woman who found her pony in a snowdrift after the great blizzard of 1891, soaking wet and very cold. She rubbed his face with her apron and gave him a drop of brandy, 'an' he luked up in my vace za pittice-like and bevered tu mouth like a Cursthan'. DA 1885, 1891, 1900, 1962 and 1983 all include the word.

Blackbutter, laver, DA 1895.

Blackdoctor, the five-spotted burnet moth, DA 1928.

Blackworm, blackbeetle, WR. DA 1895 and 1897.

Blake-away, to faint, WR. According to DA 1884 a child at the end of a spasm of whooping cough 'blakes away', and FE, JP, SH all have 'blaking, crying till out of breath'. DA 1912, 1941 and 1945 give examples of 'blake' in the sense of fainting or being reduced to exhaustion after a fit of laughing or crying.

Blazee, to fly into a rage, FE. SH: 'blazing, shouting in a loud voice, to spread abroad'.

Blenking or blenk, to snow: see 'blink'.

Bless vore, to use charms and spells, FE.

Blid, blood, but also a decrepit person or someone deserving of pity: 'poor old blid', poor old soul.TM, RC, WR, MF, SH, JS. DA 1913 and 1940.

Bliddy-pot, black pudding, WR.

Blindmares, twaddle or deception, JP. The word is used in this sense by Patty in H.J. Daniel's 'Roger and Patty'.

Blink, a spark of fire, but also to snow. JP has ' anything flaky — snow or floating ashes'. However FE defines 'to blenky or blenk' as 'to snow but sparingly' while WR and SH have 'blunk, a spark'. DA 1884: 'blanks'.

Blogging, bloggy, looking sullen, FE, JP, WR.

Bloody warriors, wallflowers, JP, SH (spelling it 'bliddywaryers'), HW, DA 1931 and 1981.

Blooth, blossom, JP, WR, SH. DA 1910.

Blowmaunger; FE says this word was used by Exmoor people 'to denote a fat blown cheeked person'. JP: 'a fat pursy person'.

Boneshave, sciatica, FE, JP, WR, ON, SH, DA 1931

Boostering, labouring busily in a fussy, bustling manner; working hard enough to sweat, FE, JP, WR.

Bosky, tipsy, WR.

Bowerly, blooming, comely, 'a bowerly woman', TM, JP, WR, MF. DA 1886 and 1927.

Boys love, southernwood, JP, WR, SH.

Brandires, brandis, a trivet, FE, JP, WR, SH. DA 1911.

Braund, broan and other spellings, a billet of firewood, FE. WR 'braun, the yule fire-log', SH: 'a log of fire-wood'. DA 1878: 'brawn, Christmas fire-log'.

Brimmels, brambles, WR, SH. DA 1909, 'brimble'.

Briss, or briss and buttons, sheep's dung, FE. JP: dust, rubbish. WR 'briss, brist, breeze, dust'. MF: 'small twigs from a wood rick used for lighting fires'. DA 1909: 'briss, dust or small bits of furze'. DA 1934: 'bris, broken pieces'.

Brit, to indent, JP, RC, WR, SH.

Brownkittee, bronchitis, SH, JS.

Buckard or bucked, milk soured by being kept too long in a bucket, or in a dirty bucket, FE. JP gives 'bucked' for both sour milk and strong cheese. SH: 'bucky', sour. DA 1877. (DA 1939 however gives 'buck, cheek, rudeness')

Buddled, drowned, suffocated: FE, WR. JP gives both 'buddle, to suffocate' and 'buddled, drunk'.

Buldering, sultry, hot (of weather): FE, JP, WR, MF. DA 1884, both 'boldering ' and 'boldering clouds'.

Bullbagger, a scarecrow, anything or anyone causing a scare: WR, SH. DA 1939.

Bullums, sloes, SH, DA 1928.

Bungy, short and stout: SH. DA1877.

Busky-eyed, drunk, SH. DA 1921 has simply 'busky, drunk'.

Butt, a word with a number of meanings. JP gives three — cart, fishing basket and beehive. WM shows it as denoting several sorts of cart: 'a close-bodied cart, or wheel cart; gurry butt, or sledge cart, ox-butt, horse-butt'. TM and WR both give it as 'a close-bodied cart'. SH omits the definition of cart and instead has both beehive and kneeling pad. DA 1885 has 'hedge'. DA 1911 has 'face to face' ('He meet 'em full butt'). DA 1932 has 'hassock'.

Butter and eggs, *narcissus bifloris*. JP; jonquils, WR.

Butter rose, primrose. WR.

Buzznacking, fussing, fidgeting. DA 1886.

Buzzom-chucked: from 'bassam'.FE has buzzam-chucked, red checked.

By Goodger, an oath (By the devil) WR.

C

Cab, sticky substance, cold sweat, hence cabby: JP. SH, 'a piece of dirt adhering to plates or dishes, or to other materials'. DA 1889, 'cabby, sticky, dirty, messy'. DA 1952, 'cab-a-dab, a messy person.

Cabbical, capital, very good, SH, JS.

Caddel, *(Heracleum Sphondilum sic)* cow parsley, TM. *(Heracleum Sphondylium* is now known as Hogweed, while Cow Parsley is *Anthriscus Sylvestris).*

Caddling, loafing about, SH. DA 1897. DA 1936: 'caddling round, pottering about'.

Candle teening, candle lighting, FE, JP, RC, WR, JS.

Caniffle, to dissemble and flatter, FE.

Car, carry. 'Car'd to vant' (carried to font or baptized). RC, SH, JS. DA 1884, 1897.

Carmantree, axles and wheels without carriage, WR.

Cat-handed, ungainly, fumbling, FE, WR.

Catteball, ball such as children play with, MF. SH: 'kaddy-ball, tennis ball'.

Caucheries, medicinal mixture: FE. JP: 'cauch, a disgusting mixture or mess'.. MF: simply 'mixture'. WR: 'kautch, a disagreeable mixture'. SH has both 'cautch, mess' and 'cautcheries, medicines'. DA 1880, 1889, 1921 ('cauchy'). DA 1991: a meal of left-overs fried or boiled in a stew, generally an unattractive mess.

Cave of potatoes, clamp, JP. DA 1915.

Caw, liver fluke in sheep, JP. WR: 'cawed, diseased as in sheep'. SH: 'diseased'. DA 1879 'cawd, rot, disease of sheep'; DA 1982: 'cawthed, of sheep with lung disease'.

Cawbaby, an awkward, timid boy, WR.

Cess or zess, a mow in a barn, TM, WR. DA 1990: 'recess, corn placed in a barn in a small mow before threshing'. SH however has 'cess, happiness'.

Chad, cham, chave for 'I had', 'I am', 'I have'. FE says he thinks the 'ch' form of 'I' is entirely obsolete and forgotten in the district, and suggests that its use in the 'Exmoor Courtship' and 'Scolding' is much exaggerated. Yet evidently Sarah Hewett, Sir John Fortescue amd others did not think so. TM gives the pronunciations 'sham', 'shave' and 'shell'. 'Chall' is cited in DA 1893 and 1908. and 'chev' in 1879.

Chaynee-eyed, squinting, SH.

Chilbladders, chilblains, JP, RC, WR.

Chimmer, chimber, bedroom or upstairs room, RC, SH, JS. DA 1878.

Chingstey: FE says he never heard the term applied as in the text of the 'Exmoor Scolding', but that the leather strap which fastens a horse's bridle by passing round the jaw is called a chin-stay.

Chockling, cackling of a hen when disturbed, also scolding: FE, SH.

Chongy, changeable, unsettled, stormy, applied to weather: FE.

Chrisemore, an unchristened child, a poor creature, JP, WR.

Chuer, a job of work (evidently a variation of 'chore'). Several spellings occur in the glossaries: WR, 'chewer'; MF, 'chewers, odd jobs'; SH, 'chure, char'. DA 1882, 'own household work, chewers'. DA 1883, 'chore, work-job'

Chuff, churlish, surly, JP. SH: ill-tempered. DA 1891.

Claggy, viscous or clammy, TM ('the potatoes are claggy'), MF. WR gives 'close, cloggy, glutinous, waxy'. JP has 'claggy, viscous or clammy' and SH 'cledgee, sticky'.

Clam, a log as a makeshift bridge, FE. DA: a narrow footbridge. DA 1995: a clapper bridge.

Clapper-claw, an enraged woman, JP. SH: 'to scold'.

Clavel, a chimney piece, FE. JP: 'clovel, cross beam of a mantelpiece'. SH: 'clovel, the beam in a chimney'. DA 1881, 1936 and 1978 have similar definitions with different spelling.

Clitty, close, clotted, TM. WR has both 'clitty, close, clotted' and 'clit-bread, heavy bread, not raised'. MF: clitty. SH: 'clit, heavy'. DA 1885: 'clit, heavy or sodden'. DA 1893, 1909 and 1921 have variations. DA 1997 gives 'clitch' not only as to stick together but also to clutch or seize.

Cloam (sometimes clome), earthenware: FE, TM, WR. MF, SH, HW. DA 1879: 'cloamen'.

Clouted shoes, shoes shod with iron at toe and heel, JP.

Coad, caud, unhealthy, common disease in sheep, FE: see 'caw'.

Cob, mud or loam with straw, TM. WR: 'mud or loam mixed with straw for building'. SH: 'a dry ball of earth'. (Cob, as a building material for cottages and barns, was of course in use for centuries in the west of England.)

Cockleart, daybreak, FE. JP: 'cockleary, daybreak'. WR and JS, 'cockleert, cocklight, dawn'.

Codglove, a hedging glove, FE, WR.

Coltee, to act the hobbyhorse, to be playful as a young colt, FE. JP: 'colter, to be skittish, to play the hoyden'. WR: 'colting, frolicking as a colt'.

Condiddled, dispersed, FE. WR's version is 'to convey away secretly', whereas Pulman, in 'Job's Patience', apparently uses the word in the sense of afflicting.

Conkabell, an icicle, FE. RC: 'cockabel'; WR 'conkerbell'; SH: 'conkerbil'; JS: 'conkible'. DA 1910, 1924, 1928, 1976 and 1977 similarly give varied spellings.

Coochy-handed, left-handed, 1889: see 'cuchy-pawed'.

Copperfinch, chaffinch, WR.

Corniwillin, the lapwing, WR.

Cousin Betty, a female who goes about the country to excite charity, TM.

Cowflop, foxglove, JP, RC. TM called it 'cowslip', and WR 'cowslop'. DA 1884, 1891 and 1976. DA 1938 pointed out that other names for this flower are flopdock, floppy dock, pop-dock and purples.

Cracky, a wren, WR. This little bird, like the titmouse and others, had many names in the Devon dialect, as Richard Chope's 'Bird Names' shows; they included crackety, cutt, cutty, cuddie, cuddie-bum, cuddley, kittitop, tidley, tidley-tope and titty todger.

Crams, creases, fidgets, SH. JS: 'foolish habits, ridiculous or unaccountable ideas or sayings'. DA 1877: 'cram, to crease, to disarrange'.

Crap-full, chock full or replete, JP.

Creem, to squeeze, to press together, FE, JP, WR. MF: 'creemed, shivering'. SH gives both 'to shiver' and 'to mash'. JS has 'flesh creeping'. DA 1889: 'to feel chilly' and also 'to hold tight, to squeeze'. DA 1994: 'to shiver, to mash and to squeeze'.

Crewdling, cold, dull, inactive or sickly, FE. WR: 'crewdle, to gather up yourself. To 'crewdle auver the vire'.

Crewnting, grumbling or complaining, FE, WR. JP: 'crewsling, complaining without cause'. DA 1952: 'crusling, grumbling'.

Cricket, a low four-legged stool, JP. WR and SH: a three-legged stool. DA 1911 and 1925.

Crime of the country, report of the neighbourhood, FE, JP, WR. DA 1902.

Croud, a fiddler, hence crouder, a fiddler, FE. JP, WR: 'crowd'. SH: 'crowdie' to fiddle'.

Crub, crumb of dry bread, FE, JP, WR, SH. The word is also defined as 'a trough for feeding horses in a stable'.

Cruel, used in the sense of 'very', as 'cruel hard', 'cruel fast', etc: JP, TM, RC, MF, SH.

Cubaby, a ladybird, WR.

Cuchy-pawed, left-handed, SH. DA 1877: 'coochy, awkward'. DA 1887, 1889 amd 1913, left-handed. DA 1961, coochy, left-handed.

Cuckold buttons, the burrs of the burdock, WR.

Cuff a tale, exchange stories, FE. WR: 'exchange stories as if contending for mastery'. DA 1923: 'cuff, a chat, conversation'.

D

Dabberdashed, soiled, DA 1878.

Dallylaw, a spoiled child, SH.

Dap, a tap, a gentle knock, WR; to drop quickly, a sharp slap, SH, HW. DA 1925:a tap, blow. However, the word is used by ON and JS as 'to move quickly'. DA 1910 quotes the latter in this sense.

Daps, likeness, FE: 'the very daps of one, the exact likeness in shape, or manners'. T M, RC, WR, SH, JS. DA 1897 spells it 'dapse'.

Dashel, thistle: FE, JP, WM, TM, WR, SH, HW. MF spells it 'dicels'. DA 1897.

Davered, faded, JP, RC. MF: withered. SH: 'divered, dead, faded'. DA 1902: 'dabbered'; DA 1983, 'divered'.

Dawcake, a silly person, SH; dawcock, a silly, awkward fellow, WR. HW uses 'dawbake' for a fool, and DA 1933, 1937 and 1983 give either dawbake or dawcake for a stupid person.

Dere, to hurry, to frighten or astonish a child, FE. WR: 'to hurry, to frighten'.

Dern, see 'dorns'.

Derrymouse, dormouse, WR. DA 1926, 'dottymouse'. DA 1929, 'dorymouse'. One of Edward Capern's 'Lays for Little Ones' begins 'Little dotty derrymouse, Sleeping in your tiny house.

Rounded like a ball.'

Dildrams, to talk strangely, FE. JP: improbable stories'. WR: 'dildrums, childish nonsense; to tell doldrums and Buckingham Jenkins, to talk wildly'. DA 1936 gives 'didrums' as meaning nervousness.

Dimmet, dimmits, dimpse, dimpsy, dimpity, dimpty: FE, RC, WR, SH, MF, HW, DA1884, 1885, 1902, 1909, 1975 and 1983 all give some variation of the word for dusk or twilight.

Dirsh, a thrush, TM, WR. SH and DA 1900: 'drishel'.

Dishwasher, the water wagtail, JP, MF, SH. TM and WR: 'dishwater'. DA 1884, 1885, 1983.

Discoose, RC and DA 1889, bad language or angry speech.

Docity, gumption, knack, handiness, FE. WR: 'do-city, aptness, knowledge'.

Doil, to tell doil, to talk as though delirious, FE. JP: 'to tell dwale, to talk or mutter incoherently'. WR: 'to talk distractedly, to talk deliriously as in fever'. SH: 'doiled, silly'. ('To tell doil' occurs three times in the 'Exmoor Scolding').

Dorns, doorposts, FE. WR: 'durn'; MF: 'derns'; SH: 'durns'. DA 1889,

1981.

Douse, chaff, JP, WR, MF (also spelled doust and dowst.) SH: 'husks of oats or wheat; dowsty poll, a head covered with flour or dust'. See 'fowst'.

Dowl, the devil, FE, WR, SH. JS spells it 'dowell'. DA 1934 gives 'dowel' in the usual sense of a pin of wood or metal.

Drabbited, bad-tempered, SH.

Drang or drangway, a narrow passage, JP, WR, HW, JS. SH; 'drangway'; similarly DA 1897, 1981, 1996. MF defines it as 'ditch'.

Drashel, dreshel, a flail, WR, SH, HW.

Dreckstool, lower part or sill of door, JP. The word is variously spelled by WR, MF, SH, JS, DA 1889, 1932, 1963 and 1980 — drexel, draxel, dreskal, druck-stool, etc.

Dring, a crowd, TM. RC: to crowd; WR: to throng, to squeeze and 'dringst, a crowd'; MF: dringle, a throng or crowd; SH: 'dring, to crowd, to push'.

Drudge, a large team rake, TM, WR. The latter also has 'dradge, a bush harrow'. DA 1893: 'druge, a stout horse-rake employed in raking peat'.

Drumbledrane, a bumblebee, JP. WR: 'dumbeldrane, drone bee, idle person'. SH and DA 1929: 'bumblebee'. DA 1976: 'like a drummledrane in a cowflop'.

Dwale, to tell dwale, to talk or mutter deliriously, JP. FE has 'dwallee, to talk incoherently, as when drunk'. SH: 'dwalee, to talk inconsistently.' DA 1877: 'dwall, to talk incoherently, to mutter, to be delirious'. This appears to be a variation of 'doil', above.

E

Eart one, eart t'other, now one, then the other, FE, TM, WR.

Eaver, rye grass, WM. WR: 'ever or every grass' and also 'hayvor seed, grass seed'. DA 1881, 1885;

DA 1938 'evor'.

Eaving, becoming moist, DA 1889.

Elsh, new, 'an elsh maid, an uncouth girl', TM and WR.

Eth: TM observed that 'Eth, the termination of the third person singular of verbs is in use, as are hath and doth.' HW and JS show them as still in use in the early 20th century.

Ewe, wild rose: DA 1948. See 'yew brimmel'.

Ewte, to pour out, FE. TM and WR have 'eute'.

F

Fadge, to fare ('How d'ye fadge?'), TM, WR.

Fainty, close, oppressive, SH. DA 1885.

Fair or fairy, a squirrel, WM. DA 1961: 'fairy, weasel'. DA 1919 has the more usual spelling, vair, for a weasel.

Fakement, a muddle. SH.

Fantysheeny, extremely fanciful, SH. JS speaks of 'fanty sheeny old crams' in *Ole Biskit*.

Fern web, *Scarabeus Horticola,* small chafer, WR. DA 1939.

Ferrol, frame of a slate, JP. SH: 'forrel, the cover of a book'. DA 1877, 1897, 1924, 1929 all have various spellings of the word in the sense of the cover of a book.

Few, used in the sense of a small quantity of liquid ('a few broth'), RC, WR.

Fillyloo, an uproar, SH, but DA 1953 has 'pillyloo, rumpus, display of indignation'.

Fineney, to mince ('Zit down to table good now; don' ye fineney zo') TM. WR: 'finey, to mince, to pretend gentility'.

Fitchhole, a polecat, FE. SH and JS ''fitch, a stoat'. HW: 'fitchey'. DA 1927.

Fitty, clever, TM. See 'vitty'.

Flapdock, a foxglove: see also 'cowflop', etc.

Flibbits, tiny pieces, JS and DA 1911. (In the song 'Tavistock Goozey Fair' the horse 'kicked the trap to flibbits'.)

Flickermayte, mixture of milk and flour, SH, DA 1891.

Flickets, blushes, RC, RC, WR, SH.

Flink, to shake out or off, WR. SH: 'to sprinkle'.

Flip about, to move quickly, and flippant, nimble, SH, ON, JS, DA 1911. DA 1996 has 'of sticks, pliable, whippy; of persons, quick, nimble, lively'.

Flittermouse, a bat, DA 1911.

Flowernat, a flowerpot, WR; SH: a flowerbed. DA 1898. DA 1971: 'vlower knot, a flower pot or flower bed'.

Flusy-faiver, influenza, RC.

Force put, under compulsion, RC. DA 1877, 'foce-put, a necessity'.

Foreright, straightforward, honest, plain, TM, WR.

Forth, out of temper, TM, WR. DA 1917, forthy.

Foust, dirty, but also dusty from winnowing of corn, FE. JP: 'fouss, to soil'; WR: 'fowsty, dusty'; SH: fowsty, musty'. DA 1893: 'foust, to soil or befoul'.

Fozy, a titbit, a choice delicacy, JP. SH: 'frawsy, a treat, a dainty feast'.

Frightened, not alarmed but used in the sense of agreeably surprised, SH. JS: 'surprised, taken aback'. DA 1887.

Frith, brushwood, WM, TM, WR.

Fulch or fulk, to squeeze, JP. WR: 'fulch, a push,. a blow'. DA 1939, to push roughly, to shove.

Fump, the gist, the cream of the joke, JP. However, WH gives 'fump, a slap' and TM has 'frump, the upshot, the principal matter'.

Furze chat, stone chat, MF.

Fustiluggs, a big-boned person, FE; a gross unwieldy person, JP; a big-boned person, TM and WR.

G

Gaffer, galfer, goffer, grandfather and old man, WR; also gammer, gommer and grammer, grandmother and old woman.

Galagantin, large and awkward, MF.

Galdiment, a great fright, TM, WR.

Gall or gally, to frighten, JP, JS, and gallied, frightened, FE, WR, MF, SH, JS, DA1889 and 1934. DA 1935: 'galled, vexed, disappointed, irritated'.

Gallibagger, a bugbear, FE and JP (latter also has 'bull-beggar'). DA 1939 'gally-bagger, a scarecrow', but DA 1961 calls it a 'galligawk'. Strangely, SH gives 'a person fond of gadding about' for gally-bagger. JP gives 'galliment' for scarecrow.

Gammerels, lower hams in animals, undersides of the thighs in human beings, FE. JP: 'gammerells or gambils, lower hams of an animal'.

Gammet, fun, merriment, JP. WR, a game, a little sport. SH: 'gammeting, frolicking'.

Gammuts, games, SH, JS.

Gapesnest or gapesness, a wonderment or strange sight, FE. SH: 'gapnistering, staring idly about' and 'gapnest, to idle'.

Gawk, a fool, JP. MF: a stupid person. SH: 'gawkim, a fool' but also 'gawked up, sitting in a very high place'. JS has gawk, a fool and both 'gaked up, perched up, as on a pedestal' and 'gake, to stare vacantly'. DA 1938, 'gake' and DA 1940, 'gawky, awkward, ungainly'

Geowering or jowering, brawling or quarrelling, FE. TM: 'geowering, quarreling, "geowering and maundering all the day", scolding, grumbling'. WR: 'geowering, quarrelling'.

Giglet or gigleting, a silly woman laughing at nothing; a man who is good for nothing, FE; a laughing romp or tomboy, JP; a young girl full of fun, SH, who also has 'giglet market, a market where maid-servants are hired'. TM: 'giglot, a female laughing and playing wantonly'. DA 1908 notes that giglet's markets were held on the first Saturday after Lady Day.

Gladdie, yellow hammer, JP, WR. SH gives 'gladdie, a fool' and 'gladdy, the yellow-hammer'. MF calls the bird a golden gladdy. DA 1887, 1920.

Glam, a wound or sore, FE. JP: 'a wound, ulceration'. DA 1883 calls it 'relapse, second attack of illness'.

Glidder, ice, WR. JP has 'a-glibber, slipping'. In *The Labouring Life* HW claimed to have invented the word. DA 1893 says glidder was 'a glaze on earthenware, or other surfaces, but gives as an example 'The rawds waz all a-glidder, from frost.'

Goodee, to improve or get on, FE. SH has 'goodied, benefited'. DA 1878 has 'gooded' and DA 1931 has 'goody' as a verb.

Googer, the devil, WR. SH: 'goodger'.

Gooly cup, buttercup, WR.

Goose-chick. gosling, RC. DA 1931: 'guze-chick'.

Gooseflop: yet another name for the foxglove, WR. DA 1912.

Goyal: DA 1961 has 'goyle, stream in a valley bottom' and DA 1981, 'narrow ravine'. HW uses the word to mean a small combe, as does ON.

Gregories, *narcissus pseudonarcissus,* JP.

Greybird, the thrush, WM, SH, HW, DA 1939.

Greysidaisy, the daffodil, SH. DA 1889 'gracie-daisies' and DA 1910 'grassy daisies'.

Grizzlemundy, a laughing fool, one that grins at everything, FE. JP: 'one who perpetually laughs without cause, a stupid oaf'. SH: 'grizzlee, to laugh derisively'. DA 1924, to titter.

Grute, earth or stock, WR. Groot-field, ploughed field, RC. MF has both 'grute, earth' and 'grute-field, ploughed field'. DA 1909: 'groot'.

Gulge or gulk, to swallow voraciously, JP. MF: 'gulging, drinking' and 'gulk, to swallow'. SH: 'gulging, drinking greedily' and also 'gulk, to drink quickly'. Used by H.J. Daniel in 'Roger and Patty' and by JS.

Gurry butt, a dung cart, WR. See 'Butt'.

Guttering, eating greedily, FE, SH and DA 1881.

H

Hackmal, tomtit, SH. See 'ackymal' for variations in spelling.

Hadgeboar, hedgehpg, WR. MF: 'hedgaboor'. DA 1912: 'hedge-a-boar'.

Haggage, a slattern, FE. WR: 'hagegy, untidy'. SH: 'an untidy woman'. DA 1891, 'hagagin, untidy in dress'.

Haidge-traw, hedge trough or ditch beside road, JS.

Haigle, hawthorn berry, WR. Alternatives cited by RC are aggles or aigles.

Haimses, part of horse collar, WR.

Hamlet. See 'Amlet.

Hanje or hange, intestines (lights, heart, liver), FE. SH: 'the purtenance of sheep'.

Hangallus, hang gallows, good for nothing, impudent, ill-behaved, JS.

Hapse, to fasten, latch or bolt, WR, RC, JS.

Haveage, race or lineage, WR.

Haydigee, in high spirits, frolicsome, TM, WR.

Heal or hell, to cover with slates; also hellier, a slater, TM. JP, RC: 'hailing, slated roof'. WR: 'hail,to cover, hailing stones, roof slates'. SH: 'hale, to cover up'. DA 1884, 1898, 1921. (DA 1887 has 'cover of a book')

Henavoreday, like a hen awakened in the night, bemused, wool-gathering, dreamy, inattentive, JS. DA 1991, 'fussing with little result'.

Hend, to throw, TW. WR: 'to hand over, to throw'. SH: 'henn, to throw at'.

High-de-lows, boisterous merry-making, JP. SH: 'vulgar actions'.

Holm screech, missel thrush, JP, MF, SH. DA 1893, 1930, 1980.

Hood, wood, WR, MF.

Hoodwall, green woodpecker, MF. DA 1889.

Hoop, a bullfinch, JP, TM, WR, MF. DA 1889

Hookem-snivey, deceitful actions, SH.

Horry, mouldy, FE, JP.

Horse-snap, knapweed, JP (included by RC in his 'Devon Plant Names').

Hozeburd, a term of mild abuse, SH, JS. DA 1934 spells it 'hosebird'.

Hulsander, the white ash, WR.

Hucksheens, the hocks, the hams, FE. RC: 'huxons, ankles;. WR: 'hux, huxen, the hock bone'. In H.J. Daniel's 'Roger and Patty', Roger is greatly excited by a glimpse of Patty's huxens 'vraped in white stockings'.)

I.

Icybells, icicle, MF. DA 1929. See 'conkabell'.

Ile, beard of corn, DA 1883. WR: 'hile, the beard of barley'. SH: 'barley-ile'.

Ilt or elt, a gelt sow, FE.

Items, tricks, fancies, caprices, JP. RC: 'iteming, fidgety'. WR: 'items, fidgets'. SH: 'item, trick' and 'itemy, full of tricks, uncertain of behaviour'. JS: 'items, foolish tricks, pranks' and 'iteming, fooling'. DA 1878, 1887 and 1956 have similar definitions.

J.

Jacketawad, *ignius fatuus,* FE. SH spells it 'jackie-woad'.

Jakes, mess, SH. WR: 'jaques, filth'.

Jaykle, Oh Jaykle, interjection, JP. JS: 'jaly, exclamation'.

Jit, an upward twitch, a push, a sharp slap, SH. JS: 'to knock, push or nudge'. DA 1877: 'jet, jerk'. DA 1928: 'slight push. nudge'.

Johnny-come-vortnight, a pedlar, hawker, JS. DA 1932, 1981.

Joney, an ornament, SH. DA 1889: 'joanie, a small china figure'. DA 1961: 'joanies, any china ornament'.

Jonic, truthful, honest, SH. HW and JS spell it jonnick. DA 1884 has 'pleasant, agreeable, easy to get on with'. DA 1922: 'honest, fair dealing'.

Joulter-head, blockhead, JP.

K.

Keezer, a kind of sieve, WM, TM.

Keiger, a cask, WR.

Keive, a mash tub; also a mound of earth in which mangolds or potatoes are stored for winter use, SH. WR: 'a large tub for fermented beer'. DA 1927: 'keeve, a corn bin, box or hutch'.

Kerping, carping, finding fault, FE. SH: 'kerpee, to find fault'.

Keslings or gristlings, wild plums, SH.

Kex, dry stalks. Some plants, as hemlock, are called kexies, TM, WR. Also given in Richard Chope's 'Devon Plant Names'

Kibbit, a short thick stick, a cudgel, WR. DA 1939.

Kicketh, stammers, MF.

Kickhammer, a stammerer, FE, JP, SH. DA 1925.

Kickshaw, an entertainment, exhibition, amusement, JS — whereas DA 1938 has 'an untidy, unfashionably or oddly dressed person, an oddity'.

Kittibats, a sort of buskins or gaiters, JP, WR.

Kitty-tope, the wren, DA 1887; DA 1914: 'kiddly-tope'. See 'tidly-tope'.

Kootch, coarse grass, SH. The usual spelling, 'couch' is used by HW and others.

Kutch-pawed, left-handed, DA 1893. See 'cuchy-pawed'.

L.

Lablolly, a silly person, SH.

Lairy, faint for want of food, DA 1890 and 1982. See 'leary'.

Lathing, an invitation, FE, WR.

Lattin, iron plated with tin, JP. WR and SH have 'tinned plate or platter'. DA 1905: 'a latten cup, a tin cup'.

Leaping stock, mounting block, JP. WR: 'epping stock, mounting steps'. See also 'upping stock'.

Leechway, the path in which the dead are carried to be buried, FE. JP: 'leachway, lichway'. SH: 'leechway, the path to a graveyard'.

Leery or leary, empty, unladen, hungry, FE, WM, RC, WR, SH, JS, DA 1900. DA 1922 says that it might be used to mean unemployed. DA 1954 gives it as 'depressed'. DA 1993: 'empty, hungry'.

Leatherbird, a bat, WR.

Lent rose, daffodil, WM.

Lerruping, a flogging, WR. MF: 'lerrup, to chastise'. SH: 'larrup, to beat' and also 'larruping, gaunt and untidy'. DA 1937: 'lerrup, to walk fast'. DA 1969: 'lerruped, hit'. DA 1970: 'lerrup or lirrup, an awkward, clumsy or ungainly person'. DA 1971: 'lerrupers, big strapping things'.

Limeash floors, referred to by various writers. HW, in *Tales of a Devon Village,* said that such floors were made of gravel from the beach, washed to get out the salt, mixed with the ashes of slaked lime and a quart or two of cider, and trodden underfoot 'until all the air bubbles were broken out of the hardening mass'. Constant wear gave it a hard, polished surface.

Limmer: 'I'll lay my girdle about your backside if I catch 'ee 'eaving stones at my door agen, you young limmer, you', HW, *Life in a Devon Village.* DA 1919: 'an unruly, mischievous child'. DA 1923: 'rascal, scamp', DA 1991: ''Twas a limmer', referring to a bad pain. DA 1997, a term of personal abuse. However TM has 'Limmers or timbers, shafts', WR has 'limmers, joints' and also friends, acquaintances, connections.

Limperskimp, wild celery sought by horses when ill, WR. In 'Devon Plant Names' Richard Chope gives it as cowparsley.

Linhay, an open shed, WM, TM, RC, MF, SH, HW.

Logic, much talk, possessing more sound than sense, JS. DA 1883: 'nonsense'.

Longcripple, an earthworm, WR. MF: a lizard. SH: a viper. HW: a slowworm.

Loblolly, used for a sloppy food — junket, blancmange, syllabub etc., FE. SH: 'spoon meat'.

Loplolly, lounging, not firm, WR.

Lustree or lewstery, to bustle about like a sturdy woman, to work hard, FE. RC: 'louster, to work hard, to labour'. MF and SH: 'lowster, to work laboriously'.

M

Make-wise, pretend, FE. WR, MF: 'make believe'.

Malley, donkey, WR. RC and MF spell it mulley.

Malls, measles, FE, JP.

Mallywallop, a tall untidy woman, SH.

Mang , to mix, TM, WR.

Maskell , a caterpillar, WR. SH: 'malscral'. DA 1885, 1902, 1960 and 1980 give various spellings — mahl-scralls, molscrols, mascal.

Masterpiece, something remarkable or unusual, HW, JS. DA 1892 and 1916.

Maur, a root, TM, RC, MF. SH: 'mores, roots' and also 'moar-an'-mewl, root and branch' and 'moot, or mute, root of tree'.

Mawguts, sheep's intestines, RC, DA 1897.

Mawn, a wicker basket with two handles, WR, DA 1888.

Mazed, mad, crazy, FE, WM, WR, MF, HW. SH: 'mazedheaded, dizzy'. DA 1911.

Mazed finch, the wagtail, SH.

Maygames, frolics, SH. MF: 'magames (sic) nonsense'.

Meach off, to play truant, FE. TM: 'meech'. WR and SH: 'mitch'. DA 1891 and 1895 give variations in spelling.

Mewstaddle, a stone on which mows are set and mewstead, stackyard, WR. DA 1991: 'moostidge'.

Mimpsy-pimpsy, dainty, SH.

Mixen, a dunghill, TM, WR, DA 1917.

Miz-maze, SH: perplexity. JS, DA 1953 and 1982.

Moily, labour like a mule, FE.

Mommet, a scarecrow, SH. JS: 'puppet, doll, scarecrow'. DA 1975, 'naughty child'; DA 1997, 'an obstinate, obtuse or awkward person, also a mischievous child'.

Moody-hearted, melancholy, JP. WR: 'weak-hearted, dispirited'. SH: 'muty-hearted, sensitive'. JS: (who also uses 'mully-'arted) 'soft-hearted, easily touched, cowardly'. DA 1910 and DA 1914.

Moot, to root out, TM. WR: 'rooting out and the roots themselves'. MF: 'to root out'. SH: 'root of trees'. JS: 'stump and root of a tree'.

Mort, lard, WR, SH. JS: 'a large number or quantity; also lard'.

Mopper, a handkerchief tied over head and under chin, JP. DA 1902: 'a bandage for the face'. MF: 'mopt, blindfolded'.

Mowhay, stackyard, WM.

Muggard, sullen or displeased at a real or imagined affront, FE. SH: 'muggatee, sullen'.

Mugguts, intestines, SH. See 'mawguts'.

Mullygrub gurgin, meal grub feeding on coarsest kind of meal, FE. SH: 'mullygrub, an ill-natured person'.

Mumchance, keeping silent, FE. SH: 'mumpchance, heavy in wit'. JS: 'remaining silent'.

Mux, mucks, mud, FE, JP, RC, WR.

My hyvers (also 'my eymers') my goodness, JS. DA 1995: 'my eymers, my heavens'.

N.

Naish, delicate, RC, SH. DA 1883, 1934, nash, soft, dielicate.

Narrowstaples, erysipelas, RC.

Natomy, skeleton, RC. DA 1878: 'notomy'.

Nickling, taking short steps, SH.

Niddick, the nape of the neck, FE, JP, RC, WR, SH, JS. DA 1909 and 1983.

Ninnihammer, foolish person, WR, SH. DA 1921: ' a state of nervousexcitement and expectancy'. DA 1938: 'a foolish person, one without any gumption, a simpleton'.

Nimpingang, nymping gang, a whitlow, JP, RC, MF, WR, ON, SH. DA 1890, 1917, 1980.

Ninniwatch, vain hopes or fears, FE, JP.

Nissel-tripe, the smallest of a litter, SH. WR: 'nestledraught, last born'. DA 1982: 'nisseldraf, the weakest member of a litter or brood'.

No-ti-no, (not that I know), ON, JS. SH: 'no-tany-by'. DA 1911.

Northering, wild, incoherent, TM, WR.

Nug, a bunch, JP. SF.

Nummet or nunch, small bit, TM, WR, ON. DA 1931 and 1980: 'nammet, the meal about 10 a.m.'

O.

Oaks, clubs in playing cards, JP, JS.

Oakweb, cockchafer, JP, WM, SH. WR: 'oakeb, oakem, cockchafer'. DA 1922: 'oakworm;' DA 1939: 'oakweb'; DA 1976: 'oak-ubs, large furry moths'.

Oavis, the eaves of a house, FE. JS: 'orfis'; DA 1911: 'oaves'.

Oozle-pipe, windpipe, WR. DA 1893: 'ooze'; DA 1927: 'ezel-pipe, the throat'.

Ordained, intended, WM. Much used in that sense by JS. DA 1898, 1975.

Organs, pennyroyal *(mentha pulegium)*. WR, MF. SH includes 'organtay, a decoction of pennyroyal'.

Ount: according to FE, this does not imply relationship; simply denotes an old person.

Outride, a commercial traveller, JS. DA 1933.

P.

Palch along, to walk softly, but to palch clothes is to patch or mend them, FE. Similarly SH has 'palsh, to walk slowly' and also 'palshing, walking slowly, patching clothes, untidily'. JP has simply 'palch, to walk slowly'.

Panking, panting, FE, WR, MF, SH, JS.

Pauch, paunch, to handle in unseemly manner, WR. SH: 'paunch, to handle unnecessarily'. DA 1920.

Peart, saucy, brisk, impertinent, JP. RC: 'brisk. lively'. WR: 'sharp-witted, dapper'. SH and ON, 'sprightly'.

Pigs' loose, pigstye, JP, WR, MF, JS. DA1893.

Pilgarlic, a person worthy of pity, SH. DA1940: 'a wishy-washy person, slummocky, awkward and unkempt'.

Pilm, dust raised by the wind, FE, JP, TM, RC, WR, MF, SH. DA 1897 and 1898: 'pillum'.

Pilth, fluff, SH. DA 1887.

Pindy, mouldy, musty, JP, MF, SH. DA1882: 'pindey, smell of tainted meat'. DA 1939: 'pindey, stale, tainted'.

Pingzwill, a boil, FE, JP, WR. SH: 'pinswill, a boil, a fester'. DA 1878: 'pinzwill, small abscess'. DA 1991: 'pingwill, a blackhead'.

Pinikin, delicate, JP. SH: 'pinnicking, wan, pale'. DA 1935: 'pinnicking, small, undersized, insignificant'.

Pintap, on top of, used frequently by JS (sometimes 'pon top'). DA1910.

Pittice, sorrowful, JP. SH: 'pittice, feeble'. DA 1887: 'pittish, small, mean, miserable looking'.

Pity-hole, a grave, JP. DA 1893 and 1948 have 'pit-y-hole'. In the old rhyme, 'Many nits, many pits, many slones, may groans, many aggles, many cradles', pits evidently refers to graves. HW found that village boys in Georgeham in the 1920s spoke of graves as pits.

Planches, planching, floorboards, JP. WM: 'plancher, a chamber floor'. RC: 'plaunchen vloor, wooden flooring'. SH and ON: 'planches, board floors'. DA 1900.

Plim, to swell, to increase in bulk or to make anything swell by heating, FE. SH: 'to increase in bulk'. DA, various dates, give similar definitions. DA 1983 has 'to rise, of bread, etc.'

Plum, light, JP. WM: 'light and fluffy, as some soils. RC: 'soft'. WR: 'light, soft, springy, puffy: plum soil, plum bed'. SH: 'warm, comfortable'. HW recorded that Georgeham villagers spoke of the soil being 'plum' in spring. The word is defined in seven volumes of the DA Transactions in the 1890s.

Ploskett, a water meadow, JP. SH: 'plasket, a quagmire'.

Poochee, pout or screw up one's mouth, FE. JP: 'pout'. WR: 'pouchy, pouting'. SH: 'pouting lips'.

Pook, a hay cock, FE, MF. SH: ' a mound of hay or turf'.

Potee, kicking when lying down, FE. WR: 'to throw one's legs about'. SH: 'to kick about in bed'. DA 1887, 1923, 1924.

Puggen end, gable end of building, JP. DA 1887, 1920. Used by H.J. Daniel in 'Roger and Patty',

Pumble-foot, club foot, WR. SH: 'pumble-vooted, malformation of foot'. JS: 'pummle-vooted, lame'. DA 1910: 'pummle-vooted, lame, limping'. DA 1971: 'pumble-toed, pigeon-toed'.

Putch, pitching hay or corn, usually loading a wagon or haystack, FE. However it is used in the Devon lady's dialect letter (chapter four) in the sense of 'to sit down': 'He ax'd us to putch'.

Q

Quail, queel, to faint away, WR. DA 1925. (However DA 1923 has 'fit to be cut for hay').

Quarrenders, red apples peculiar to Devonshire, ON, SH.

Quat, satisfied fully, RC. JS: 'quatt, flat, squat, deflated'. DA 1940: 'to press, squeeze flat, crush'. An alternative spelling, 'quott', is given by FE to mean weary of eating and also to sit down, while SH defines it as 'to sit on the haunches'.

Quelstring, hot, sultry, FE (who also includes 'squelstering weather, sultry weather'). SH: 'quelstring, sweltering'.

Querking, groaning, grunting, complaining, FE, WR. SH: 'querking, grunting' and DA 1914: 'quirk, to grunt'.

R.

Ragrowstering, romping, frolicking, FE. (It is spelled 'ragrouting' in the 'Exmoor Courtship') SH has both 'ragrowstering' and 'rowstering' as 'romping'. HW.

Ramakin, thin, WR.

Rame, to stretch oneself and also 'rames' a thin person, WR, MF. SH: 'rayme, to stretch' and 'raymes, a thin person, a skeleton'. DA 1878: 'bony remnants, the skeleton'. By contrast, JP has 'rames, dried stalks of beans, peas, etc.'

Rant-a-come-scour, clamorous scold or man in a fury, JP. SH: 'ranticomescour, an uproar'. DA 1892: 'at a great rate and making a great noise'.

Rare-mouse, a bat, JP. DA 1910: 'rary-mouse'.

Ream, to stretch or strain, FE. MF: 'reamed, stretched'. See 'rame'

Reed mote or reed mott, a pipe of straw, WR, HW.

Rexens, rushes, FE, SH, JS, DA1881.

Rigg, an impudent wanton girl and rigmutton-rumpstall, a wanton, FE, who also defined the many uncomplimentary names for women included in the 'Exmoor Scolding': rouzabout, a rough, slapdash, bustling hoyden; rubbacrock, a filthy slattern; swashbucket, a slovenly woman who splashes pigs' food out of a bucket, trapes, a slattern and trub, a slut.

Rory-tory, tawdry, MF. SH: 'very gaudy'.

Roundshaving, abusive scolding, FE, SH.

Rowl, real and also revel, FE, who adds that 'Nearly every village in the district still has its revel, when a kind of rustic fair is held, with wrestling, bell-ringing and much drunkenness.'

Rucky, to crouch, FE, WR, SH. DA 1919, to stoop. DA 1889, 'ruckey-down, to stoop'. DA 1914: 'crucked up'. DA 1976: 'crockey down, squatting down'. DA 1995: 'crecky down, to crouch; also croopy down'.

Ruge or ruse, slide down a slope, JP. RC: 'ruzement, a landslip'. DA 1889: 'rouseing away, crumbling'. DA 1897: 'aroozed down, slid down'. DA 1992: 'roozer, a cliff fall'.

Rummage, nonsense, SH, HW, JS. DA 1936: 'rubbish, litter, odds and ends, of little or no value'.

S.

Sam-sawed, half-cooked, WR. See 'zam-zawed'.

Sar, to earn, to serve, FE, TM, RC, WR, SH, JS. DA 1994.

Sart, soft, softly, JP. WR spells it with an initial 'z', which would have been the usual pronunciation, as with many other words beginning with 's'.

Scad or scud, a shower, MF. FE: 'scat, a shower'. SH has both 'scads, passing showers' and 'scats, dashing showers'. JS gives 'scat' as a word of many meanings — 'shock, shower of rain, bewildered, separated, broken'. HW uses it to mean hit. DA 1997: 'fling, or a passing shower'.

Sclum, to give long scratches with the nails, SH.

Scoochy pawed, left-handed, awkward, WR. See 'cuchy-pawed'.

Scummer, to smear, to clean indifferently, WR. SH: 'skummer, mess'. JS: 'fuss, bother, confusion'.

Scute, a tip, RC, a gift, MF. SH: 'skute, a reward'. JS: 'a great deal of money'.

Sewl or zule, a plough, WM. Various spellings: FE has 'zowl', WR 'zole' and DA 1899 'zull'. DA 1956, 1979.

Shab off or away, skulk away ashamedly or unobserved, JP, SH, JS, DA 1975.

Sheerymouse, a bat, MF, DA 1921.

Shool, a shovel, FE. JP: 'showl-a-mouthed, shovel-mouthed or capacious'. SH: 'showl, a shovel'. DA 1887, 'Put to bed with a showl': buried.

Skaredevil or skir, a swift, WR. (TM has 'skir, a swift, a black martin'.)

Slammock, an untidy person, WR. SH: 'slammicking, untidy'. JS: 'slammicking, untidy; slammicking about, walking sluggishly'. DA 1886.

Slottery weather, rainy weather, FE. WR: 'slotter, to spill'. MF: 'slottering, dirty, wet'. JS: 'slatter (sic) to spill, slop'. DA 1920.

Smeech, smitch, smirch or blacken with smoke, JP. Smoke, WR. MF: 'offensive smell in the fire'. SH: 'dust, smoke' JS: 'choking smoke or dust'. DA 1961: 'smitch, smoke'.

Snartlegoggs, snartlegoggers or snarligogs, blackbeetles or cockroaches: DA 1920, 1931, 1953.

Soce or soace, companions, mates, FE, who suggests that the word is a vestigial survival of the monkish *socii,* brethren. JP claimed that 'soce or zoce' was falling into disuse. For WR it meant friend, companion, and SH similarly said it meant 'good friends'. RC's suggestion that it meant 'indeed' is clearly incorrect. The definition given by JS, 'a friendly, sociable form of address to include everybody present ("come, soce, sit down. Supper's ready")' is evidently the best, although of course the word could be used when addressing only one person. H.J. Daniel's spells the word 'sossee' in 'Roger and Patty'.

Souant, fair, even, regular, WM and TM. See suent.

Spud, a good spud: a good gift or legacy, FE.

Spudlee, to bestir oneself, FE. JP: 'spuddle, to kick,, rake or stir the ground, like chickens'. RC: 'spuddling, stirring (literally scratching the ground, but used for fussing about'). SH: 'spudlee, to stir about'. JS: 'spuddled, pottered about, meddled with things'. DA 1967: 'to scratch about'.

Standry's Fire, erysipelas, RC.

Steehopping, fond of gadding about, FE. JP: 'gadding, gossiping, romping up and down stairs'. WR: 'stayhopping, giddy, wanton'.

Stewardly, like a good housewife, FE. JP: 'sturdly, thrifty, housewifely'. MF: 'stewardly, managing, "a good stewardly wife"'.

Stewer, a dust, a fuss, WR and SH. (FE has 'sture' for dust.)

Stivering, standing stiff, FE. WR: 'stiver-powl, bristle-headed'. SH: 'stiver, to tousel'. DA 1991: 'stivered up, to tousel or disarray'.

Stroil, strength, agility, FE. There seems to have been some confusion between 'stroil' and 'sproil'. WM has 'stroyl, couch or other weeds', TM has 'stroyl, couch grass or other weeds, raked out of the soil', MF has both 'sproil, strength' and 'stroil, grass weeds' and WR has 'stroile, strength, also couch grass'.

Strub, picked, RC. WR: 'to strip or take away everything'.

Stub, a good stub, a large sum of money, FE and JP. SH: 'hoard'.

Stubberds, delicious apples, SH.

Stuggy, short and thick, applied to a little boy, JP, WR, SH.

Suent, even, regular, JP. WM and TM spell it 'souant'. WR: 'suant, even'. MF: 'suent, even, smooth'. ON: 'suant'. SH: 'suent, smooth'. JS calls it 'an admirable word and a great loss to the common language'. DA 1886, 'evenly, smoothly'.DA 1910, 'even, level'. DA 1971, 'proper'.

T.

Tack, a slap or smack, FE, WR, SH, (TM has 'tack, a shelf'). DA 1931 'tack, up to standard'. DA 1839, 'a ledge or shelf".

Tacky-lacky, a person at everyone's beck. SH. DA 1929, maid of all work.

Tallet, a hayloft, FE. TM: 'a garret, a room next the roof'. RC: 'a hayloft'. WR, SH, HW, JS, a loft.

Tankerabogus, a bogie, SH. (JP has 'tantarabobs or tantarabobus, the devil')

Tantara, a disturbance, MF. SH: 'tantara, an uproar'. (DA 1921 gives 'tantaro' for bearded wheat.)

Teehoss, to romp vulgarly, SH.

Teen, to light or to close, JP. ('Candle-teening' appears in the 'Exmoor Scolding'.) WR: 'tine, to shut or close'. SH: 'tine, to shut to' and 'tyne, to close, to tie, to extinguish'.

Telling, talking, conversing, RC, ON. JS: 'tell, as a verb, talk — "He'll tell by the hour if anybody will harken to 'en"; as a noun — "Let's sit down and have a tell for a minute"'.

Terrifying, annoying, nothing to do with alarm, JS. DA 1911, 1961. DA 1996: 'terrify, surprise, astound, astonish'.

Therle, gaunt, thin, FE. WR: 'thurl, thin'. SH: 'thurdled, meagre, thin'. JS: 'thurdle-gutted, thin, starved-looking'. DA 1939, 'gaunt, lean, hungry looking'. DA 1887 'thurdle, miserable, wretched.

Thurt, across, athwart; thurt-eyed, cross-eyed, JS. See also 'athert'.

Tidly-tope, a wren, MF, SH and DA 1921. SH: 'tidlee, tidlee-tope, the wren'. (MF has 'tidly-goldfinch, gold-crested wren'. See also chapter seven.

Tiffes, light downy particles, JP. WR: 'tiefil, a filament; tiefilled, untwisted'. SH: 'tiffels, detached threads'. DA 1923: 'tiffell'.

Tiltish, ready to take offence; of a horse, apt to kick, FE. TM and WR: tilty, testy, soon offended'.

Timersome, sensitive, shy, timid, FE. WR: 'timmersome, timorous, fearful'.

Tinkeraments, ornaments, odds and ends, JS. SH: 'trinkums, silver articles, jewellery'.

Tino, tino-by, certainly not, SH, ON. DA 1961: 'tan-e-bye, not that I know by'. See 'no-ti-no'.

Toad: not of course a dialect word, but much used in Devon, as JS amusingly emphasizes in his glossary to *Ole Biskit*. 'Almost everything living is a toad at some time or another. The baby's a bright little toad, Jimmy's a trying toad, Polly's a careless toad, father's an unlucky toad, grandfather's a knowing ole toad, the rooks be terrifying toads, the cat's a thieving toad, and the toad's a frog'. In DA 1960, a Dartmoor man, offered sympathy on the death of his wife, replied 'Oh, daun 'ee be zorry 'bout thaat, the Lord be welcome to 'er, 'er was a terrible tayjiss ole tawd'.

Tongtree, the pole of an ox cart or wagon, WM. TM spells it 'tangtree'.

Totle, a slow lazy person, FE. JP: 'totle, a loiterer or imbecile'. DA 1994: 'totalish, of an old person, childish, simple-minded'.

Toze, unravelling, untangling, FE. SH: 'to shake a feather bed, to comb wool'.

Trade, a generic word, equivalent to 'stuff', as green trade, garden trade, doctor's trade, etc. RC: '"stuff" of any kind'. WR: 'trash'. SH: 'leavings, rubbish.' Also used by ON. JS remarks that it 'stands for any commodity of which we can't readily supply the name: "They dished up some old trade that I wouldn't give to a cat"'. DA 1925: 'a term of disparagement'.

Trapes, a slattern, FE; a slut, WR; an untidy woman, SH.

Trindle, a salting tub, WR. SH: 'trundle, a salting tub'.

Try (How do you try? How do you do, how are you?), FE. 'How do you try, How do you do?' JP. 'How d'ye try; How do you get on?' WR.

Twobill, a two-headed tool, WR. SH: 'tubill, twibil'. DA 1900, a double-headed mattock. DA 1992, 'tooble, a two bill, a mattock with a digging and an axe head'.

U.

Umps-ouze, almshouse, SH. DA 1936 and 1997.

Unket, dreary, dull, lonesome, TM, WR.

Upping stock, stone steps from which to mount, ON, SH. See 'leaping stock'.

Upzetting, upsitting, a gossiping or christening feast, FE. JP: 'a debauch or gossip at a neighbour's'. WR has simply 'christening'.

Upright, exactly the hour (upright vower, exactly four o'clock') JS, and DA 1922.

Upstore, an uproar, SH. JS: 'tumult, riot, disturbance'.

V.

Vad, the beam of a cider press, TM, WR.

Vady, tainted, SH. DA 1889, damp; DA 1932, steamy; DA 1981, tainted.

Vang, to take or seize; also formerly to act as a godfather at a christening, FE. JP: 'to take or receive' but also 'bang'. WR: 'to receive, to raise money'. MF: 'to take money'. SH: 'to stick close to' and also 'vang-to, to act as sponsor'.

Veaking, fretful and peevish, FE, JP and SH. WR: 'veag, ill temper'.

Vell, to separate turf from the soil, TM and WR. The latter also has 'velling plough for taking off turf'.

Vinnied, mouldy, FE. WM, TM and MF all give 'vinny' as mouldy. WR: 'vinhed, mouldy, as cheese.' SH: 'vinnied, mouldy, bad-tempered'.

Vittee, to go well or successfully, and also vitty, decent, fitly, well, FE. WM has 'vetty, apposite, suitable'. TM: 'vitty, suitable, neat'. WR: 'vitty, fitting, proper'. MF, like TM, has 'vitty, suitable, neat'. SH: 'vittee, fit, proper'. DA 1971: 'viddy, tidy' and also 'vitty, sprightly'.

Visgy or bisgy, a mattock, SH. See 'bisgee'.

Vlother, incoherent talk, nonsense, TM, WR.

Vorrage, earth collected for 'melling' with lime, WM.

Vump, a thump, FE. JP: 'vump, knock or thump; vumping, great'. SH: 'knock'.

W.

Wab, tongue,SH.

Wallage, a lump, JP. WR: 'a large quantity'. SH: 'an untidy bundle'. DA 1936 and 1970: the latter has 'wolage or wollage, a large helping, a heap'.

Wangary or wangery, soft and flabby, FE and WR. SH: 'limp, weary'. DA

1927: 'limp, flabby, tired'. DA 1962: 'wan, limp and lifeless'.

Want, a mole, TM, WM, RC, WR, SH, DA 1889. According to Richard Chope, a familiar pun used by mole-catchers before beginning work was 'I've come to supply my wants by catching yours'.

Wardship, a wagtail, TM, WR.

Washdish, a wagtail, WR.

Watter-swate, clean, SH. DA 1891, smelling sweet after washing.

Waxing curls, swollen glands of neck, SH.

Wee-wow, unsteady or wavering, FE. SH: 'crosswise, puckered, squinting'.

Whappet, a blow with the hollow of the hand, FE.

Wherret, a slap or cuff, FE.

Whisterpoop, a whistling blow, a sudden blow, FE. SH: 'a backhand slap'; she gives the same definition for 'whisterclister'. MF gives a 'a box on the ear' for 'whistleclister'.

Whitpot, milk, flour and treacle, WR. SH: 'hasty pudding'. JS describes it as 'white pot, a dish formerly made with milk, now applied to insipid or trivial talk, or discourse which is beyond the understanding of the hearer'. DA 1889: 'nonsense'. DA 1936: 'nonsense, foolish talk'.

Widdy-waddy, foolish, rather weak, RC. DA 1913: 'changeable'.

Wildego, a harum-scarum person, WR. DA 1910, 'wildy-go, unruly'. DA 1979, 'said of an unruly child'.

Wimb, wimbing, wimly, to winnow, WR, SH. HW records seeing a wimbling machine in an old barn in Georgeham in the 1920s. DA 1936, DA 1971.

Windle, a fieldfare, WR. MF: 'windell, a redwing'. SH: 'winnels, thrushes'. HW, DA 1867, 'red-wing'. DA 1991.

Winnicky, used by HW as Georgeham opinion of his behaviour. DA 1991: 'winnicky, weak, feeble'.

Wipswile, every few minutes, SH. JS: 'now and then, at short intervals'. DA 1950 and 1960 (the latter spells it 'wippiwile').

Wish, inapt, bad, unfit, as "wish weather", WM and TM. RC: 'wisht, poor, dismal, pitiable'. WR: 'wist, dismal'. MF: 'sickly, ill'. SH: 'pallid, sickly, white-faced'. JS: 'wheesht, uncanny, ghostly, sickly-looking'. HW: 'weest, dreary'.

Woodquist, wood pigeon, TM, WR.

Wug! word used by carters and others when they wanted their horses to turn left, JS and DA 1911. (To turn right the command was 'Come 'ere!')

Y.

As Devon speakers often modulated words beginning with an aspirate to a 'y' sound, some glossary writers included many words spelled with an initial 'h' under 'y': yaffer for heifer, yaw or yeo for ewe, yearth for hearth, yeth for heath, yetting for heating, yurdle for hurdle and so on. Both WR and SH include these. MF, SH and JS all have 'yark' in the sense of sprightly or sharp witted; DA 1883 has 'lively' and 1913 'sharp, knowing.' WR gives 'yarreth, yarrow', 'yen, to throw or hand over', 'yewbrimmel, dog rose', 'yusen, a trough to feed cattle from, attached to a cow house, but also a dung heap'. (DA 1971 has 'yewmat, wild rose' and DA 1991 'yous'n, a manger'.)

Z.

Zamzawed, meat overboiled or parboiled, JP, MF, HW. RC: 'zimzad, boiled until too soft'. SH: 'zamzawd, sodden'. DA 1889 'zam-zody, soft, damp, wet'. DA 1900: 'zam-zaway, half-baked, of dull intellect and also zamzoaky, tepid, applied to tea. DA 1975: 'zim-zam, overcooked'.

Zar, zart: see sar and sart.

Zayhaddick, valerian, WR.

Zess, a pile of sheaves in a barn, FE, WM, WR. DA 1937.

Zawk, a silly person, SH.

Zigg, urine, FE.

Zim, to seem. 'I zim' means 'it means to me; not 'I seem'. RC, SH, JS. WR: 'zem, to seem, to seem pleased with'.

Zive, sive, a scythe, FE, WR.

Zogging, dozing, JP, MF, SH. DA 1932: 'zog, a short nap, snooze'.

Zole, zowl, zull, a plough: see 'sewl'.

Zoundy, to swoon, T M.

Zour-zab, a sour-tempered person, after sour apple, SH, JS.

Zowerswopped, ill-natured, crabbed, FE.

Zugs, bogs, soft places, 'like a cow in the zugs', stuck fast unable to move, JS.

Zwop, noise of something falling or (as in the 'Exmoor Courtship') a smacking kiss, FE.

Appendix Two

1.Widecombe Fair, traditional

2.Tavistock Goozey Fair by C John Trythall

3.A 'appy-go-lucky old chap. Anonymous.

4.Bitzvord Justis by Edward Capern

5.Out Come Mother and Me by Jan Stewer. (A.J. Coles) and choruses from When Mother and Me Joined In and What about a Little Drop of Cider?

Widecombe Fair is perhaps the best known of all Devon folk songs. That this was so even in Victorian times is shown by the fact that when the Rev. Baring-Gould appealed in local newspapers for readers to send him songs, all he received were versions of 'Widecombe Fair'. Just when it was written, and by whom, does not seem to be known.

The words and music of the less lugubrious 'Tavistock Goozey Fair', first published in 1912, are given as by C.J. Trythall. Enquiries at Tavistock and Plymouth libraries and the Music and Drama department of Exeter Central Library have not produced any information about Trythall, and his name does not appear in Grove's *Encyclopaedia of Music.* Yet this lively song gives the impression of having been based on a genuine folk original. Is it possible that Trythall merely set down words he had heard somewhere and arranged the tune in a publishable form?

Widecombe Fair

Tom Pearce, Tom Pearce, lend me your grey mare,
All along, downalong, outalong lee,
For I want to go to Widecombe Fair,
Wi' Bill Brewer, Jan Stewer, Peter Gurney,
Peter Davy, Dan'l Whiddon, Harry 'Awk,
Old Uncle Tom Cobleigh and all,
Old Uncle Tom Cobleigh and all.

And when shall I see again my grey mare:
All along, etc.
By Friday soon or Saturday noon,
Wi' Bill Brewer, Jan Stewer, etc.

Then Friday came, and Saturday noon,
All along, etc.
But Tom Pearce's grey mare her hath not trotted home,
Wi' Bill Brewer, etc.

Tom Pearce's old mare her took sick and her died,
All along, etc.
And Tom Pearce he sat down on a stone and he cried
Wi' Bill Brewer, etc.

But this isn't the end of this shocking affair,
All along, etc.
Nor, though they be dead, of the horrid career,
Of Bill Brewer, etc.

When the wind whistles cold on the Moor of a night,
All along, etc.
Tom Pearce's old mare doth appear gashly white,
Wi' Bill Brewer, etc.

And all night long be heard skirling and groans,
All along, etc.
From Tom Pearce's old mare and her rattling bones,
From Bill Brewer, etc.

Tavistock Goozey Vair by C John Trythall

Tiz jist a month come Vriday nex'
Bill Camperdown an' me
Us draiv'd acrass aul Dartymoor
Th' Goozey Vair t'zee
Us maade ourzel's quate viddy
Us shaved an' graized our ayer
Then off us gaws een our Zindy claws
Be'ind Bill's auld grey mare.
Us smelled th' zage an' onions
Aul th' way vrom Whitchurch Down
An' did'n us 'av a blaw out
When us put up een town
An' there us met Ned 'Annaford
Jan Stewer an' Nicky Square
An' it zimmed to me aul Dem mus' be
T' Tavistock Goozey Vair.

Chorus:
An' it's aul an' wer be gwain?
An' what be doin' ov ther'?
'Aive down yer prong
An' step down 'long
T' Tavistock Goozey Vair

Us wen' t'zee th'osses
An' th'effers an' th'yaws
Us wen' pun aul th' round'bouts
An een t'aul th' shaws
An then it started rainin'
An blawin' too, ees fay
Zo off us gaws up to "Th' Rawz"
T'av a dish o' tay
An' ther' us ad a zing zong
An' th' volks kep drappin' een
An' they wat naw us all come round
An' 'ad a drap o' gin
Till wat wi' one an t' other
Us didd'n zim t' care
Whether us wuz t' Bellever Tor
Or Tavistock Goozey Vair.

Chorus:
Ver wer' an what be doin'?, etc.

T'wuz rainin' strames an' dark as pitch
Wen us started awm that night
An' wen us got pass Merrivale Burge
Th' ole mare 'er took'd t'vright
Zed I t' Bill, "Be careful
Or yu'll 'av us een th' drain".
Zed Bill t'me "Be dad t' thee
Why — am'n yu got th' reins?"
Jist then th' aul mare er rinned
Agin a wackin' gert big stone
'Er kicked the trap t' flibbets

An''er tratted off alone
Wen us cumm'd to us reckon'd
Twadd'n naw gude zittin' ther
Zo us 'ad t' trudge awm vourteen mile
Vrum Tavistock Goozey Vair.

Chorus:
Ver wer' an what be doin'?, etc.

A 'appy-go-lucky Ole Chap

I was born in a rare lucky time
Last year o' the cen'try an' all,
The last month and day, hour and minute volks zay,
Else I never should been born at all.

A mewlin' and pukin' young brat,
I crawled out of bed for a lark,
Valled flat on me back and killed a gurt rat
Who was aitin' o' me milk in the dark.

When older they putt me to schule,
To taich me vor raid and vor write,
The more of the schule the bigger the vule,
All I larned was to swaer and to vight.

Zo they putt me to work on the varm
To larn vor to plough and to zaw;
Couldn't get a lot varder, vor even me vather
Couldn't tell me what I didn't knaw.

Vor sport I can tell 'e a tale.
Wan morning I walked 'cross tha Bray,
It made me quite shiver when out of the river —
Me boots vull of trout vit to fry.
Up cross the Gurt Meadow I went
Climbed up a tall bank wi' me hands,
With each of the pair I gripped a gurt hare,
I'm tellin' 'e just as it stands.

I got to a round baley rick
Wi' pigeons all thick in the thatch,
'Twist me gun round me lags, and shut round the sags
Zo killed all the birds wi' one snatch.

I nex' bought a varm wi' no cash
Wi' timber drawed in as an ort,
Timber then went up top, and I cut down the crop
An zo had me ole varm for nort.

I've lived yer vor all one long live
A merry-go-lucky ole chap,
No man's enemy — no man's friend d' 'e zee?
Zo write me this yer epitaph
Epitaph
I was married when ighty an' ight,
Just ninety and nine when I died — o!
An' now I don't care, vor I've had all me share
Zo fel-deldel-didly-i-do!
Chorus
A 'appy-go-lucky ole chap
No matter what pace I do go,
I yer volks zay
He'll be merry alway
Can't zee why 't shouldn't be zo.

Bitzvord Justis by Edward Capern

Edward Capern (1819-1894) was born at Tiverton. His family moved to Barnstaple when he was two years old. When he was only eight his mother became bedridden and, in the harsh conditions of the time, he had to start work. A job in the local lace factory, with long hours for very little money, impaired his sight. He had various other jobs before moving to Bideford in 1847 to become a postman, with a route extending as far as Buckland Brewer. Somehow he had managed to learn to read and write, and was evidently an enthusiastic reader of poetry. With the help and encouragement of William Rock, the philanthropic business man, author of 'Jim and Nell' as well as a great deal of more conventional verse, his first book , called simply *'Poems'* as published in 1856. It was followed by *Wayside Warbles* (1865), *Ballads and Songs* (1868) and *Sunshine and Shadows* (1881). He dedicated *Ballads and Songs* to Baroness Burdett Coutts, who had become his patron. He was awarded a Civil List pension of £40 a year, later increased to £60. Having ceased to be a rural postman, he moved to Birmingham in 1866, and lived there until 1884. However, his last years were spent in Braunton.

Although his published books contain one or two poems in Scottish and other dialects, it seems that he had little interest in writing in his native dialect. That he could do so effectively if he chose is shown by 'Bitzvord Justis' (Bideford Justice) which originally appeared in 'Tom Hood's Christmas Annual' in 1875. The version that follows was reproduced by F.J. Snell in his *Book of Exmoor.*

Gracey: Aw massey, soce! gude lawks, how be 'e?
Es yurd tha nuze tu-day?
Mally: No, Gracey, no! Hot es it, cheel?
Gracey: About owld Jerry Gay.
Mally: Just make a putch, an lit es yur
Hot tez — tha hozebird! — Wull
Es allez zed he'd niver kum
Tu enny gude mazell.
Od, drat 'n, he'th bin pauchin, Grace
Or zummat, I'll be bound!
Tha hops — he's zartin to be hung.
His like wur niver vound.
Gracey: No, Mally, et es wis 'en that.
Mally: Nan?
Gracey: Zumthin wis, Iss zay!
Mally: Hot! wis 'en pauchin, Gracey?
Gracey: Ees.
A gurt dale wis, ees vay!
I'll tell tha al about et, deame;
Yu knaw tha narra drang?
Wull, es ed jist bin up, d'ye zee?
Tu spayk way Hurchy Crang;
An wen es cum hout, Mall, agen,
The hair was lik a vilm.
"Hot iver be min 'bowt," zes I,
"Tha rawd es vule o' pilm!"
'Twore zetch a sture' es niver zeed
Tha hoi rawd zo avore —
Tha zeame ez ef owl Codden Hill

Wur tore up moot and more.
And hot de thenk twor al abowt?
'Tez tru, ez I'm alive!
Thay wur a-shakin Jerry, Mall,
For batin ov es wive.
Tu du tha theeng al viddevide,
Thay gort a blanket, deame,
An in thay shuv'd 'n, nek an crap,
An mead en ot ez vleame.
Ees, thare wur Jenny Maskell, vust;
Nex Zuke an Nanny May;
Then Honor Brooks an Dally Prist,
An strappin Becky Day,
An Varmer Zluman, he war thare!
An Taylor Jans, Iss wadge!
An Kit tha cobbler an tha Clerk;
Tha smith, tu, Josha Madge.
Pore Jerry, Iss shall scat ma zides
Tu tell ee al tha vun,
Thare he wur, tumlin upze down,
Tha gowlin zen o' a gun.
"Aw, do ee stap, an let me go!"
Ha kald hout, wen a-bump;
An up a went agen sky-hoi,
Wance more to kum down vlump!
"Yu meslin ov a brute! dest yur,
Weth tha hang-galluz lukes,
Wist iver zarve er zo agen?"
"Spake hout!" zez Honor Brooks.
"Quick, in a minnit!" Honor zeth,
"Or up ee go agen."
"No, niver, niver, NIVER more!"
Zays Jerry, zore way pain.
An zo thay let 'n hout, when, lor,
Mall, zitch a zite wur zeed!
Ha like a dug a tail-piped urn'd
Or vox et vule-kry speed.
Es laff'd tu zee Bet Zlitterpuche

An that gurt slammick, Zal,
Gie chace, an by tha scruff o' th' nek
Jist sheake tha skarekraw, Mall.
An lor ee shude a zeed tha pegs
A por, go wildago,
An Kitty Cole's owld dunkey, Jack,
Way divil-glintin Joe.
On went tha skeremouch bekeend
Down Ruckaborough Hill,
Till Jerry went tu hide-a-peep,
Zumweare ba Matha's Mill!
I'll wadge a hunderd ginneys, deame,
He'll not vorgit tha day.
Now Iss mus weesh es wull; tez time
That Iss wur on ma way.

Out Come Mother and Me by Jan Stewer (A.J.Coles)

When Mother and me was married fust 'twas up to Lunnon town
Where Susan was in sarvice too, and her missis provided the gown.
The marriage was in a butiful church where dukes all goes to wed
And crowds come around to see who 'twas with their eyes jumping out of their head

When

Out come Mother and me

Me and Mother beside one tother
Her with her hand ketched hold to mine
Stepping out so brave and fine
Out come Mother and me
As noble as could be
'Twas funny to see the people stare
Outside the church to 'Anniver Square
To see who was gwain to come out from there
And out came Mother and me.
(repeat) Me and Mother beside one tother, etc.

They waited from twelve to one o'clock

To see a Princess in a butiful frock
And a Lord at least — my days what a shock
When out come Mother and me.

Me and Mother went up to town to see the Lord Mayor's shaw
Thousands of folks was gapping like gawks when the musickers started to blaw
The sawjers come fust and then all the chariots gorgeous to behold
And then come the gurt Lord Mayor hisself in his butiful carriage of gold
And then
Out come Mother and me (repeated to 'as noble as could be)
There was effigies there of famous men
Of tableaux I counted a hundred and ten
But the loudest cheer of the lot was when
Out come Mother and me . . . .
I was never in my life so proud
Parading between the cheering crowd,
The Lord Mayor titched his hat and he bowed
And so did Mother and me.

In Muddlecombe once us got the news the King was passing through,
The folks all flocked to the station at the time the train was due,
Me and Mother had been away, and us come back on that train.
The Mayor was there to welcome the King with his hat and his gown and his chain
When out comes Mother and me.
The band striked up 'God Save the King'
The people cheered like anything
A policeman put 'em all back in a ring
And out come Mother and me.

Now once us went to a meeting where 'twas said 'Admission Free'
Fust they gave us a temperance speech and then they gived us a tea,
Us eat so much as ever us could and then they sold us a pup
The chairman said 'My friends, the collection will now be taken up' so
Out went Mother and me . . . .
Us didn't know what on earth to do
Us only had fourpence between us two

And I wanted to look in the Old Horseshoe
So out goes Mother and me . . . .
But a chap with a plate was stuck on the door
Says I 'My word, what's that on the floor?'
He turned around and with out any more
Out goes Mother and me.

Two other songs by Jan Stewer which he included in his public performances, but which were perhaps rather less popular than 'Out Come Mother and Me' were 'When Mother and Me Joined In' and 'What about a Little Drop of Cider?' The choruses of these ran as follows:

When mother and me joined in
My word, what a time we spent.
Us didn't know much of the steps may be,
But that didn't matter to mother and me.
Us made our own steps as us went.
I bowed to mother, her bowed to me,
The band beginned to play,
Then off us went with a 'One two three,'
And showed the youngsters the way.
They was begging our pardon left and right
When we began to spin.
You'd never believe the difference it made
When mother and me joined in.

What about a little drop o' cider,
Just to make the wheels go round?
What about a little drop o' cider,
You'll be better for it I'll be bound.
Whether you're a walker or a rider,
Fill your mug up once before you start.
What about a little drop o' cider,
Just to warm the cockles of your heart?